SWEENEY TODD
THE DEMON BARBER OF FLEET STREET

Mark Salisbury

Foreword by Tim Burton

With Extracts from the Screenplay by John Logan

Music and Lyrics by Stephen Sondheim

Based on the Musical by Stephen Sondheim and Hugh Wheeler

Originally Staged by Harold Prince

From an Adaptation by Christopher Bond

Executive Producer Patrick McCormick

Produced by Richard D. Zanuck   Walter Parkes   Laurie MacDonald   John Logan

Directed by Tim Burton

TITAN BOOKS

Attend the tale of
Sweeney Todd.
His skin was pale
and his eye was odd.
He shaved the faces
of gentlemen
Who never thereafter
were heard of again.
He trod a path
that few have trod,
Did Sweeney Todd,
The Demon Barber
of Fleet Street.

SWEENEY TODD

CONTENTS

Page

FOREWORD BY TIM BURTON · · · · · · 6

PART ONE: *His Skin Was Pale and His Eye Was Odd…*
Bringing Sweeney Todd to the Screen · · · · · 10

PROLOGUE: *A History, of Sorts* · · · · · · 12
FINDING SWEENEY TODD · · · · · · 26
FINDING MRS LOVETT · · · · · · · 42
FINDING THE LOOK · · · · · · · 52
FINDING A SUPPORTING CAST · · · · · 62
MAKING MUSIC · · · · · · · · 72
NO PLACE LIKE LONDON: *The Sets* · · · · · 86
EPILOGUE: *A Beautiful Marriage* · · · · · 98

PART TWO: *Attend the Tale…*
The Illustrated Story · · · · · · · 102

FOREWORD

*O*f all musicals, Sweeney Todd *is my favorite.*

The opportunity to create a film that is a combination of horror movie and musical was very exciting. It provided me with the chance to tap into the Hammer Horror films as well as the old Universal films with actors like Boris Karloff, Peter Lorre, and Lon Chaney. I believe Sweeney Todd is in the same league as characters presented in those films.

My sincere thanks to the amazing cast and crew for bringing this story to life. I hope this book gives you a proper look at the making of the film and our strange and bloody good times.

TIM BURTON

Previous spread:
Burton, seated in Sweeney's infamous chair, contemplates the darker side of Todd.

Top left:
Director Tim Burton advises his actors.

Top right:
Tim Burton in pensive mode, as Depp and Sacha Baron Cohen enjoy a lighter moment.

Bottom:
Tim Burton talks through a shot with co-producer/first assistant director Katterli Frauenfelder.

Opposite:
Burton's watercolour sketch of Sweeney Todd dispatching a victim. Bloodily.

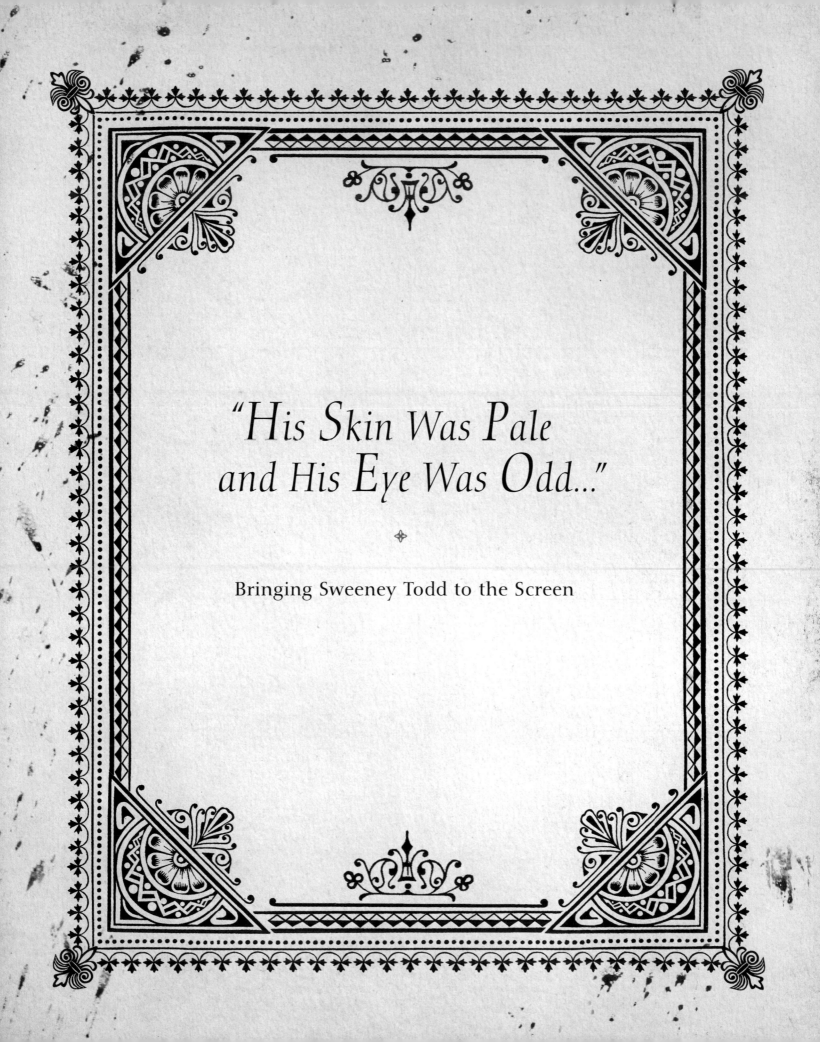

"His Skin Was Pale and His Eye Was Odd..."

Bringing Sweeney Todd to the Screen

PROLOGUE: A HISTORY, OF SORTS

The name of Sweeney Todd has long inspired fear and dread. A 19th century barber and notorious serial killer, Sweeney Todd would cut his customers' throats while they sat in his barber's chair, before sending their bloody corpses down a specially made chute and into the cellar, where they were chopped up by his accomplice in crime, the baker Mrs Lovett, and used as the filling for her meat pies.

While author Peter Haining claimed in his 1993 book *Sweeney Todd: The Real Story of the Demon Barber of Fleet Street* that Todd actually existed and was responsible for around 160 murders in 18th century London, it's more commonly accepted that he was, in fact, a fictional creation who first came to prominence in a story called *The String of Pearls: A Romance* written by Thomas Peckett Prest and published in November 1846.

From that initial appearance in *The People's Periodical*, a Victorian Penny Dreadful, the Todd legend quickly grew. A year later the story was adapted into a play that bore the subtitle *The Demon Barber of Fleet Street*. And soon, Sweeney Todd's notoriety was almost rivaling that of another 19th century London serial killer – Jack the Ripper.

The Sweeney Todd story has inspired a number of stage productions down the years, as well as films for both the big and small screens, notably George King's 1936 black and white *Sweeney Todd, The Demon Barber of Fleet Street* starring the aptly named Tod Slaughter (who continued to play Sweeney in a touring stage version well into the 1950s), and the 1998 John Schlesinger-directed TV version, *The Tale of Sweeney Todd*, which starred Ben Kingsley as Sweeney and Joanna Lumley as Mrs Lovett. But it was playwright Christopher Bond who, with his 1973 stage production, *Sweeney Todd*, expanded the legend by introducing the revenge plot that is now associated with Sweeney's tale.

Arriving back in London after escaping from fifteen years of false imprisonment in Australia, Benjamin Barker vows to kill the evil Judge Turpin and his nefarious henchman, Beadle Bamford. It was Turpin who shipped him off to the other side of the world on a trumped-up charge in order to steal his wife, Lucy, and his baby daughter from him. Adopting the guise of Sweeney Todd, Barker sets up in his old Barber's Shop above the pie-making premises of Mrs Nellie Lovett, who tells him that his wife poisoned herself after the Judge took advantage of her. But when a rival barber, the flamboyant Italian Pirelli, threatens to expose Barker's new identity, Sweeney kills him by cutting his throat. With Todd not knowing what to do with the body, Mrs Lovett proposes a rather ghoulish solution to both Sweeney's problem and her ailing pie-making business: using human flesh as the filling for her pies.

Soon, Sweeney discovers that the Judge has turned his amorous affections towards Todd's now teenage daughter Johanna, who has become Turpin's ward. Imprisoned in his house, Johanna is, one day, noticed by Anthony, the young sailor who found Sweeney floating on a raft in the middle of the ocean, having escaped his penal servitude, and rescued him. Hopelessly in love, Anthony vows to rescue Johanna and

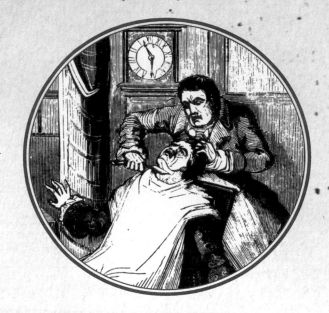

marry her himself.

Mrs Lovett's pies, meanwhile, have become the talk of London and as business booms, she dreams of respectability and a life at the seaside, with Sweeney as her husband, and her young charge, Pirelli's former assistant Toby, as her adopted son. But Sweeney has only revenge on his mind – to the detriment of anyone or anything else...

In 1979, using Bond's play as his template, legendary American lyricist and composer Stephen Sondheim – one of a very select group to have won an Academy Award®, a Tony Award®, an Emmy®, a Grammy® and a Pulitzer Prize – brought the legend of Sweeney Todd to an even greater audience, with his and Hugh Wheeler's acclaimed stage musical, *Sweeney Todd: The Demon Barber of Fleet Street*.

Débuting in New York on March 1, 1979, and starring Len Cariou as Sweeney Todd and Angela Lansbury as Mrs Lovett, *Sweeney Todd: The Demon Barber of Fleet Street* was quite unlike anything then seen on Broadway. Blood arched across the stage when Sweeney sliced into his victims, while the score – inspired by the work of renowned soundtrack composer Bernard Herrmann, whose collaborations with director Alfred Hitchcock included *Psycho* and *The Birds* – was, in places, frightening and abrasive.

While director Tim Burton didn't see the original Broadway show, he did attend an early production of *Sweeney Todd* in London

while still a student. "I loved it," he says. "I wasn't in movies, I didn't know anything about Stephen Sondheim. The poster just looked kind of cool, kind of interesting. I'm not a big musical fan but I did love it, because it's like an old horror movie. It's also such an interesting juxtaposition with the music being very beautiful and the imagery being kind of old horror movie. And it was interesting to see something bloody on stage, too. Actually, I went to see it twice because I liked it so much."

"I saw the original Broadway show three

teenager. The now-partner of director Tim Burton, Bonham Carter recalls playing the soundtrack album that her parents, who had seen the show in London, brought home. "Mum and Dad were big fans, and I remember sitting in my drawing room looking at the score, going through the lyrics and listening to it," she says. "I got completely hooked on the music. I've always loved Sondheim. He's such a genius to be able to write both lyrics and music."

But the teenage Bonham Carter's love for *Sweeney Todd* extended further than just

times when I was in high school," recalls screenwriter and producer John Logan. "The first time was their final preview, the night before they opened, and I'd never seen anything like it in my life. It was galvanizing. I fell in love with it and it's stayed with me forever. When you tend to think Broadway musical, Rogers and Hammerstein comes to mind, where people have nice little dialogue scenes, they break into a lovely little song, then the song ends and they go back into dialogue. *Sweeney Todd* starts with a horrific, howling sound on organ that shakes you to your toes. It is unsettling. It is creepy. It is genuinely eerie. The first image you see is people throwing a body into a grave, so immediately you're not in 'Bye Bye Birdie' any more! It is the only time in my life I have been genuinely frightened in the theater."

Another huge fan is British actress Helena Bonham Carter, who has been enamored by the musical since she was a

an admiration for Sondheim. "It might sound a bit sick, but since I was thirteen I've always wanted to play Mrs Lovett," she laughs. "I think a lot of kids love it because of the gore and because it is a melodrama, and there is a bit of Punch & Judy in there. And there's the myth of it and the fact that you don't quite know whether it's true or not. When I told a friend I was learning to sing to audition for *Sweeney Todd*, she said, 'Well, of course you're going to get it.' I said, 'Well, no, not necessarily.' She

said, 'No, no, no, we used to call you Mrs Lovett at school. You went around with Mrs Lovett hairdos. Don't you remember?' But I had absolutely no memory."

Given Hollywood's fondness for adapting successful stage musicals into big screen movies, it was inevitable that the film rights to Sondheim's show would be snapped up, even if the dark, difficult subject matter of *Sweeney Todd* – which, after all, involves multiple murders and cannibalism – didn't make it the most obvious choice for a cinematic adaptation. Burton had in fact first flirted with directing a movie version of it around the time of *Batman*. He recalls telling the project's then-producers that he didn't really need a script; that the music was story enough. "It's all kind of there," Burton remembers explaining to them. "You listen to the music and it tells you the story, seventy-five or eighty percent. But back then, especially at the stage I was at, [it was like] 'What do you mean, you're not going to do a script?' And it kind of went off on something of a tangent. Even now, it's not a movie that everybody's clamoring to make. It's not exactly *The Sound of Music*."

In 1997, Burton actually began the process of developing Sweeney Todd into a film with Warner Bros., but the offer to direct *Superman Lives* pulled him away from the project at that time.

Then, nearly a decade later, when the movie rights to *Sweeney Todd* had been acquired by DreamWorks Pictures, screenwriter and producer John Logan, who had co-written the script for the studio's multi-Oscar®-winning *Gladiator* as well as several other DreamWorks projects, called up, desperate to be involved. "I went after it like a rabid barber," he admits. "I said, 'Look, I have to do it, you don't understand my passion for *Sweeney Todd*. It changed my life.'"

Logan's perseverance and passion paid off and the writer, whose credits include *The Aviator*, *The Last Samurai* and *Any Given Sunday*, was hired to pen the script. But before he began writing, Logan decided to study the score first, in minute detail. "To be absolutely familiar with what the beast was," he reveals. "I spent about six months by myself studying the score backwards and forwards, looking at the original Chris

Bond melodrama versus the Hugh Wheeler book and really getting to know the music, so come the great day that I sat down with Stephen Sondheim I would know what I was talking about, and I wouldn't sound like an idiot."

To trim a three-hour stage musical into a two-hour movie clearly necessitated certain changes. "The movie has to be about telling the story and where the characters are emotionally, psychologically, spiritually, at that moment in the story, so a fair amount of work was done cutting and shaping," Logan explains. "We cut some songs completely. We decided to truncate various songs, we cut out verses, as well as expand certain areas. There are long sung sections that are very opera-like that, on stage, work incredibly well, but I thought would be very precious done in film. We also made artistic judgments [like] we don't really need this verse of this song so let's get rid of it, because on stage a Mrs Lovett and a Sweeney Todd can hold an audience with songs that go on for eight minutes because they're so entertaining it's like watching a vaudeville turn, but that just doesn't work in the movie."

Logan had initially been working on *Sweeney Todd* with another director, Sam Mendes (*American Beauty*, *Jarhead*), whose approach to the material was, he says, somewhat different. One of the first things Burton did when he came on board was to discuss with Logan the idea of putting more songs and more music back into the movie. "We went back to the musical," Tim Burton explains. "The first draft I read there was less music in. It actually had that feeling of a traditional musical, where there'd be lots of dialogue and then somebody bursting into

song. One of the great things about this is that it's very music driven. It's not as much as in the original show, but a lot more than in the draft I first read."

This almost wholly musical approach was one that Sondheim, apparently, had also toyed with himself when writing the show. "Originally Sondheim wanted to write a musical that was entirely musical," notes Bonham Carter, "music right from the start to the end and have no [spoken] words. But then he realized that wasn't going to be practical. Tim's instinct has been the same, to try and make the film more music than dialogue interspersed with songs."

One song that Burton quickly reinstated was 'Wait', which Mrs Lovett sings during the first act of the musical on stage. "Originally I had cut it, thinking we didn't really need it, that it was a place holder," says Logan, "but Tim quite rightly said, 'No, it is the only time in the show that Mrs Lovett gets to express in a gentle sort of way her affection for Sweeney Todd, she gets to soothe him and to calm him.' So it was an important color for her character. The key to *Sweeney Todd* is emotion. It is a very passionate story about a man who is wronged, who seeks revenge. And in the process of achieving that revenge, goes mad. It's about a woman who's in love with him, who yearns for him, but can't make a connection with him. At heart it's a very passionate, dark love story."

While Sondheim had final approval over director and the casting of both Sweeney Todd and Mrs Lovett, producer Richard Zanuck says he's been remarkably supportive. "Since this is his favorite and most acclaimed piece of work, he could have been difficult but he understands that we're making a movie and he has great faith in Tim," says the veteran producer, whose myriad credits include *Jaws*, *The Sting*, and *Driving Miss Daisy* as well as a spell in the 1960s as president of production at 20th Century Fox, the studio founded by his father, the late movie mogul Daryl. "Sondheim's a movie savant," continues Zanuck, who himself is no slouch at film history, having witnessed a great deal of it firsthand. "I tried to duel him one time about old movies and he knew much more than I did. He's seen every film, I think, since D.W. Griffith. He can tell you

everything. And while he hasn't been a part of the process [of filming], he right away said, 'Look you're making a movie. You make your movie.'"

"He's a formidable character," observes Burton of Sondheim. "He's very intelligent, very passionate, he's a genius at what he does, but the thing that I have really respected and felt very grateful for, is him letting it go. It's not a stage thing. It's a movie. I felt very supported by that. The other thing that impressed me and immediately made me like him was, when I first met him, he was talking to me about how he wrote this like a Bernard Herrmann score. And what's really interesting, when you take away the singing, and it happened when we were recording it, it *is* like a Bernard Herrmann score, it's really, really amazing! As soon as he said that I thought, 'I'm in, completely.'"

For Sondheim, the film offered a chance to change certain lyrics that, says Logan, "have just bothered him for twenty years and he thought this is a great opportunity to change them" as well writing new ones to tally with certain structural and narrative changes in Logan's script. For instance, during the song 'Poor Thing', where Mrs Lovett tells Sweeney what happened to his wife while he was incarcerated, or when Sweeney sings it to Anthony to fill him in, it was determined that they presented an opportunity to do something cinematic, to show that part of the story in a flashback. "So Steve wrote new lyrics to fit the images that Tim and I came up with," Logan reveals, "in terms of how we wanted to tell that story with the Judge giving her flowers, and her room being filled with flowers."

The key to writing *Sweeney Todd* was, says Logan, to write it like a horror movie. "I grew up on Hammer horror movies, on the old Universal horror movies, and that sensibility I understand very well," he

explains. "So when I sat down to write the screenplay I didn't try to write it like a great work of art, I tried to write it like a Hammer horror movie, so it would have momentum and drive, ripping through this terrifying story with the dispatch of *The Curse of Frankenstein* and Hammer's *Dracula*, and embracing the sort of black humor that is inherent in those movies."

And in the work of director Tim Burton, whose fondness for old horror movies is there for all to see in *Edward Scissorhands*, *Ed Wood*, *Mars Attacks!*, *Corpse Bride* and, in particular, *Sleepy Hollow*, which featured several Hammer horror stalwarts in the cast, including Count Dracula himself, Christopher Lee. "So we had a shorthand for talking about what we wanted this movie to be, which was always a horror movie," Logan continues. "We didn't look at it as a splashy musical. We didn't look at it as an intense character drama. We wanted to make a Hammer movie with the same momentum and energy and fun those movies always have. In our meetings, we would spend as much time talking about Peter Cushing and Christopher Lee as we would about Sweeney and Mrs Lovett, trying to find a sensibility that would reflect those movies we loved as kids and also appropriate to the seriousness of *Sweeney Todd*."

And yet, what really delighted Logan was Burton's concern with the emotional truth of the characters. "Not with cinematic effect. Not with, 'How do I do the horror shocks, how do I stage the musical numbers?' Not 'What's the look of the film?' It was, 'What's the truth to the characters? What is the story really about?' From a writer's perspective that is a heaven-sent director, because, as a writer, all you care about are the characters. What is breaking Sweeney Todd's heart or what is inspiring him, or what is haunting him? And that is exactly what Tim wanted to talk about. What does Sweeney Todd think when he looks at Mrs Lovett? What does Mrs Lovett think when she looks at Sweeney? How can we dramatize that for the audience?"

Ever since making his feature length directorial début with *Pee Wee's Big Adventure* in 1985, Tim Burton has been revered as one of modern cinema's true visionaries, a filmmaker gifted with enormous visual flair and the ability to create entire worlds on screen.

"Tim's an auteur, a visionary," says *Sweeney Todd* producer Richard Zanuck, working with Burton for the fourth time after *Planet of the Apes*, *Big Fish* and *Charlie and the Chocolate Factory*. "He takes chances that most directors are fearful of. This is a musical, which he's never done before. This is a love story. It also has lots of blood.

This is 'The Demon Barber of Fleet Street' and Tim is the only one that I know of who could take that on and not be afraid of the blood, not be afraid of the singing, and do it in a way that doesn't repel audiences but absolutely captivates and intrigues."

Born in Burbank, California, in 1958, Burton studied at the California Institute of the Arts (Cal Arts) before joining Walt Disney as an animator in 1979, working on *The Fox and the Hound* and *The Black Cauldron*. While frustrated by the company's production line mentality as well as his inability to draw in the Disney style, Burton's unique artistic sensibilities were eventually championed by several studio executives and he found himself directing a black and white, stop-motion animated short called *Vincent*, that was inspired by his favorite actor Vincent Price (who narrates

the film). The five-minute piece, a paean to both Price and Edgar Allen Poe, swiftly became a festival favorite, and Burton next directed a live-action version of *Hansel & Gretel* for the fledgling Disney Channel.

But it was to be his next film that would

become his Hollywood calling card. A twenty-nine-minute, live-action updating of Mary Shelley's classic tale transposed to modern-day suburbia, *Frankenweenie* was shot in glorious black and white and told of a young boy, Victor Frankenstein (Barrett Oliver) whose dog, Sparky, is run over and killed by a car. Inspired by his science teacher reanimating a frog using electricity, Victor brings Sparky back to life during an electrical storm with the inevitable chaotic consequences. Tipping its hat to both James Whale's *Frankenstein* (1931) as well as its 1935 sequel *The Bride of Frankenstein*, *Frankenweenie*, while never released theatrically in America, had its fans in Hollywood, one of whom was the comedian Paul Reubens, who was looking for someone to direct a feature film based on his rouge-faced child-man character

Pee-Wee Herman.

In the twentysomething years since *Pee-Wee's Big Adventure*, Burton's films – which include *Batman*, *Batman Returns*, *Planet of the Apes*, *Charlie and the Chocolate Factory*, and *Edward Scissorhands* – have reaped in excess of a billion dollars worldwide, but his bold style, macabre sense of humor, and cinematic voice have remained as strikingly creative and intensely personal, whether his films are based on a comic book character, a hugely popular children's novel or, in the case of *Sweeney Todd*, a well-respected Broadway musical.

"He is the perfect director for *Sweeney Todd*," insists John Logan. "There is such an affinity between the subject matter and Tim's style and sensibility. I think Tim Burton was born to direct the movie of *Sweeney Todd*."

FINDING SWEENEY TODD

Top:
If looks could kill: Sweeney and "friend" make their presence felt.

Opposite top:
Todd says goodbye to another victim.

Opposite bottom:
Sweeney in younger, happier times.

Typically, in most stage productions of Sondheim's musical, Sweeney Todd and Mrs Lovett are played by actors in their fifties. Burton, however, was determined to cast younger for his two leads – by at least ten years.

"It just felt that part of the energy on this was to make them a bit younger, in their forties, and have the kids be kids, so the ages were a bit more appropriate to what the story really was, and it's not a teenager being played by a thirty year–old," Tim Burton explains. "That, to me, was an energy that was very much filmic as opposed to a stage thing when you could get away with it. Again there was a fated

quality, a kind of a *Bonnie & Clyde* thing to them. I remember thinking about when Bette Davis got, not old, but just slightly older, there's a certain sadness to her, a certain emotional weight that seemed to fit this story."

Making both roles younger had other consequences, too. "He wanted to play Sweeney and Lovett so there's a potential for romance," notes Helena Bonham Carter, who would later be cast as Mrs Lovett, "and in a lot of the previous productions it's not necessarily been a romance. Mrs Lovett has always been in love with Sweeney but [Tim] wanted a moment where there's a potential that you could see this couple getting together. And, right till the end, just before he kills her, you think, 'Oh my God, he's going to accept her.' The absolute core of her is she's in love with this man who never notices her. He doesn't even look at her, except when she comes up with the genius idea of how to dispose of his bodies when, suddenly, she's visible. And she is a good partner, she's a good foil to him, because whereas he's totally introvert, she's extrovert. She's practical and, I think, a lot cleverer, frankly."

To play his Sweeney Todd, Burton only had one person in mind: Johnny Depp, with whom he'd first worked on *Edward Scissorhands*. While always considered one of his generation's finest actors, Johnny Depp's stock had skyrocketed in recent years thanks to his swashbuckling performance as Jack Sparrow in the *Pirates Of The Caribbean* films, a global box office phenomenon that saw him win his first Oscar® nomination for Best Actor (for 2003's *Pirates of the Caribbean: The Curse of the Black Pearl*). But for many, Depp's best work has been when collaborating with Burton, whether it be as the razor-fingered innocent of *Edward Scissorhands*, or the world's worst director with a predilection for women's clothing and, particularly, angora sweaters in *Ed Wood*, or a nervy detective facing the Headless Horseman in *Sleepy Hollow* or, more recently, as Willy Wonka, purveyor of fine, inventive confectionery in *Charlie and the Chocolate Factory*. *Sweeney Todd* would mark their sixth film together.

In late 2001, Burton visited Depp at his house in the south of France and gave him a CD of the Angela Lansbury stage production of *Sweeney Todd*. "He said, 'I don't know if you've ever heard this. Give it a listen,'" Depp recalls. "I gave it a listen

and thought, 'Well, that's interesting.' Then, five or six years later the question comes. 'Do you think you can sing?' And I didn't. I mean, the answer I gave him was, 'I don't know. I'll see if I can.'"

Burton didn't know for sure that Depp could sing. "I know he's musical. He was in a band," he observes. "I don't know that he ever sung in the band, I'd never heard him, but I know he's a very musical person and he plays the guitar. I knew all that. But I think I saw him so clearly as it, in a way, and I know he wouldn't do anything with me just to do it, and that's all I needed. And I just knew he could. It was a feeling I had that he could do it."

Not that Depp was any more certain about his ability to sing. "I knew I wasn't tone deaf," he says, "but I wasn't sure if I'd be able to sing any of it."

Depp had been in a band in Florida in the 1980s called The Kids, in which he played guitar and sang background vocals.

"I was the guy who would come in and sing the harmony, very quickly," he laughs of his rock 'n' roll past. "It would be all of three seconds and then I was out, and I could find my way back to the dark and continue playing guitar. So I had never sung a song. I said to Tim I'm going to go into the studio with this pal of mine and I'm going to investigate and try and sing the songs, and if I'm close, then we can talk about it, or I'll just call you and say, 'You know what, I can't do it. It's just impossible.'"

And so Depp called up his long-time friend Bruce Witkin, who had been the singer and bass player in The Kids, to ask for his help. Shortly afterwards, the pair went into Witkin's Los Angeles recording studio for what Depp calls "a little investigation, an experiment" to record some demos. "He said he wouldn't do it unless I helped him," explains Witkin. "I think instead of going in front of somebody with a piano and doing vocal warm-ups or whatever, he just wanted to go in with a friend that would be honest with him and say if he sucked or if he was great, and whether he should do it or he shouldn't. So we went to my place, drank some wine and smoked a bunch of cigarettes, and then it was like, 'Are we going to do this or what?'"

The first song Depp attempted was the haunting 'My Friends', which documents Sweeney Todd's relationship with his beloved razors. "That was, basically, the first song I ever sang in my life," he explains. "It was pretty weird and scary."

Depp, however, trusted his friend to be honest enough to deliver the verdict on whether the actor could sing on not. "I was like, 'Do you want the good news or the bad news?'" Witkin remembers saying to Depp on hearing his voice. "He goes, 'Well, give me the bad news.' And I said, 'The bad news is you're going to have to do this.'"

Before anyone else had heard the result of those early demos, however, *Sweeney Todd* had already been greenlit, with pre-production underway at Pinewood Studios, England in preparation for a February 2007 start date. Such is the box office clout of Johnny Depp these days. "Sets were being constructed. Wardrobe was being made. Commitments with other actors were being made," explains producer Richard Zanuck. "We were spending millions of dollars on the picture. Not one person on Earth had heard Johnny sing, and he's the star of the picture. Tim and I pretended we had heard him sing, but we hadn't. I always thought of a scene out of *The Player* or *The Producers*, with all the studio heads sitting around a large table with one little tape recorder in the centre. And out comes this little, squeaky voice, after they spent millions and millions of dollars! Well, it didn't happen that way."

Even Sondheim, who, contractually, had the final say over the casting of Sweeney Todd, had signed off on Depp without hearing him. All of which was a surprise to the actor. "I didn't understand any of it," he muses. "The only thing I understood was Tim saying, 'Do you think you can do this? I think you could.' Other than that, I didn't understand anything else. I didn't

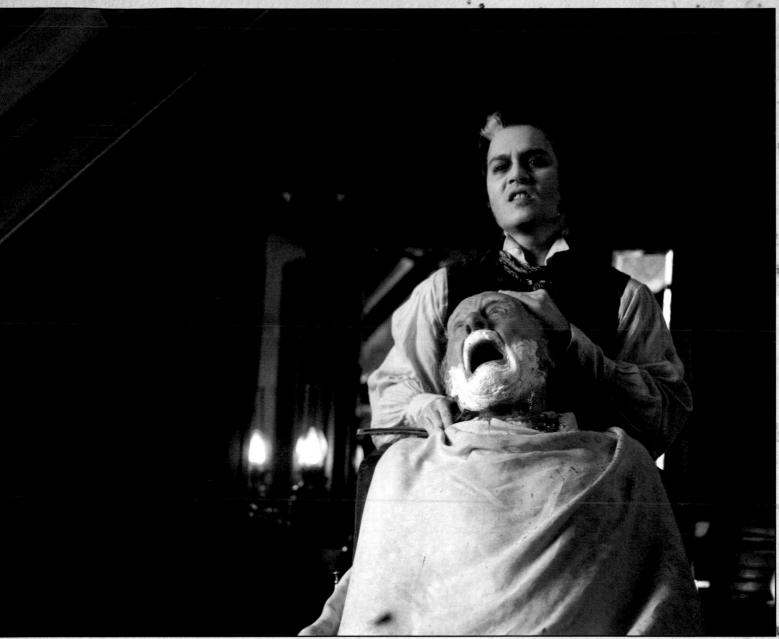

understand meeting with Sondheim and him going, 'Oh you'll be fine.' I suppose they had some kind of weird blind faith in me or were so assured that technology, even if I sang a million bad notes, would put them into a proper tune, 'cos no one had heard me sing. It was maybe a month before we started shooting [when] Sondheim's got a little listen to the demos, of one or two of the songs I'd done with Bruce."

Zanuck remembers well the day he first heard Depp sing. "I was in my office on the phone," he explains. "Tim bursts in and lays down a little cassette player and his headphones and he walks out. So I got off the phone, put them on, and listened to Johnny sing for the first time. I went into Tim's office, and we both just stared at each other with great relief. We had the biggest smiles because we knew we had a great voice with Johnny Depp, who can really pull this off. And whew! Because it could have been not so great."

"Johnny's voice is a little raspy, in the sense that it's not operatic, it's not Broadway," says Witkin. "I think he's got a little mixture of Shane MacGowan and David Bowie going on with the accent and the rasp. When we were doing the

recordings, if he cracked I would take that. If he cracked too much, I'd say, 'That one's too much,' but I tend to like stuff that sounds human and not perfect."

"He made the songs sound like they've never sounded before," observes the film's music editor Mike Higham. "I use the word accessible, because it's lovely. He's very laid back, so laid back he made the songs his own."

"It's very sexy," says Bonham Carter of Depp's singing voice. "And it sounds like him, and that's what's exciting. He really sings from the gut and it's a very emotional role. So it's very naked and very sexy and very touching and brave and beautiful, very beautiful, and soulful."

For everyone on the production, it became the most asked question from friends, family and colleagues: What does Johnny Depp sound like? Well, he sounds exactly as you would expect him to sound, with, as Witkin notes, a little Bowie, a dash of MacGowan, a smidgeon of Tom Waits and others mixed in. Not that Depp was aiming to emulate any of those singers.

"I know, not even by trying, [that] guys who you admire, come through in a way," he notes. "I mean, I wasn't going for that, but I can hear influences in there. Certainly, I can hear stuff that I might have picked up from Elvis Costello, or maybe Bowie, or Iggy [Pop]. There's a certain, weird vibrato thing that just happens. It's is an odd bird because I don't know how to sing, and suddenly the voice would start doing this waving… and you just kind of run with it, because apparently that's what your voice or your body wanted to do. And then you listen to it and go, oh wow, that sounds like this piece off of [Costello's album] *Trust*."

In fact, the role model Depp initially had in mind when he began to sing wasn't a rock performer at all, rather the late Anthony Newley, singer, songwriter, actor, and long-time Miss World presenter who had starred in a string of stage and screen musicals, including *Dr Dolittle*. "He was one of the first, main influences for what I thought might be cool for Sweeney. Then I thought that might be a little too far. Then I started thinking this is like punk, it's like punk rock. It's very elaborate, super composed, but it's like a punk rock opera, and so I started to approach it in that way, knowing that whatever voice I found for Sweeney in the demo process would more than likely be the voice he ended up with in the movie. So I heard him before I saw him, I heard him arriving."

The casting of Depp, says Logan, also gave Sweeney Todd a romantic dimension and an empathic quality that would allow audiences to accept the character, despite his murderous side. "You're asking the audience to embrace a character who is a killer, who is cold to the woman who loves him, and yet Johnny Depp makes him sympathetic," he notes. "There's something about Johnny that breaks your heart. The first time I saw him in full make-up and costume I thought, 'It's Byron!' There's something about the way he's playing the part that is so compelling you can't take your eyes off of him. It is mesmerizing to me to watch his face in close up because it manages to be romantic and terrifying at the same time – and that is the essence of Sweeney Todd, I think."

The tortured yet terrifying portrait Depp paints of Todd is of a man whose life has been utterly ruined, and is driven now by a monomaniacal quest for revenge. "Johnny is playing it with a kind of inner intensity," says Richard Zanuck. "You can see he's dangerous from the first time you

Opposite: "Sweeney's obviously a dark figure," says Depp. "But I always saw him as a victim."

see him. He's just engulfed in getting even, taking revenge upon the people that have wrecked his life, and nothing else matters. There's hardly a smile out of Sweeney but, with all that darkness and intensity, there's something fun about that too. They're making a very grotesque subject into something that is going to be very entertaining."

Having previously worked with Depp on *Charlie and the Chocolate Factory*, producer Zanuck had already experienced firsthand the actor's amazing ability to transform himself completely for a role. "Johnny Depp plays Sweeney Todd like only Johnny Depp can," he notes. "The bigger the risks, the more attractive a role is to

Johnny. He's the master of disguise. He's the master of doing something unique every time out. He has a different look, a different personality, and in this case he'll have a voice that people will be absolutely astounded about."

"The thing that's interesting about both of their careers, and both of the people they are, is they're not afraid to make choices that are a little bit outside the box," says Oscar®-winning costume designer Colleen Atwood, who has worked with Burton on eight projects beginning with *Edward Scissorhands*, and with Depp on four. "And they've both been able to do that and still be completely successful which I think for young filmmakers and people coming into

but it's all based in things that, to me, are understandable. He's a tortured soul."

In creating their Sweeney, Depp and Burton took inspiration from such iconic horror movie stars of yesteryear as Lon Chaney, Sr., Boris Karloff and Peter Lorre. In fact, it was because of their mutual love of old horror movie actors that Burton says he thought of Depp in the first place. "Because we always talk about old horror movie stars, we always thought it would be fun to do something that taps into that kind of acting style, and this had it in," Burton reveals. "Those kind of actors in those kind of movies had a certain acting style that's very much of its time but it's still very pure. If you see Peter Lorre in *Mad Love* or Boris Karloff, there's a certain primal quality to their acting that is fun to watch."

"The both of us could sit there and talk for *days* about this stuff," admits Depp. "We met at this dark little bar in New York and started thinking in terms of silent cinema, that kind of expression. Then it started coming to life; the idea of Sweeney Todd being very still, almost like a silent film character. It was very exciting. Scary."

Burton's characters are often outsiders or misfits, misunderstood and misperceived by society at large: think of Edward Scissorhands, Ed Wood, Pee-Wee Herman, even Batman, all characters who exist on the margins. And while it normally takes him several years after completing a film to fully process the personal connection he feels to them, Burton already thinks of Sweeney Todd as his favorite ever character. "He's very interior, very much inside of himself, very much in his own world, for better and for worse – mainly for worse. He's got a lot of

the industry is a continual inspiration."

For Depp, getting to the heart of Sweeney was to think of him, firstly, as a victim, not a killer. "Sweeney's obviously a dark figure," he reflects, "but I think quite a sensitive figure – hyper-sensitive – and has experienced something very dark and traumatic in his life, a grave injustice. But I always saw him as a victim. I mean, anyone who is victimized to that degree and then turns around and becomes a murderer can't all be there. I always saw him as a little bit slow. Not dumb, just a half-step behind."

And yet neither Depp nor Burton saw Sweeney as being mad. "When you've got all those emotions pent up inside of you, you could almost say anybody's a bit mad," Burton reasons. "Obviously you can look at it on the surface and say that, but I never saw it that way. He's got a madness *in* him,

demons, a lot of tragedy, that's what I loved about it."

Having the character of Sweeney Todd be almost silent (except when singing) was a throwback to many of the films Burton loved growing up, films that starred two of his favorite actors: Vincent Price and Christopher Lee. "Christopher Lee hardly spoke in the whole of *Dracula*. Vincent Price did it too, in *Dr Phibes*," Burton explains. "We kept cutting out lines in this because, unlike the stage, what's great about a film is it's closer, the actors can do things in a look. Also, it's like you can read between the lines. You don't necessarily know what they're thinking but you *see* that they're thinking, and there was something quite liberating and pleasing about that aspect of just looking at people and knowing that there's a whole bunch of stuff going on inside that you're not sure about exactly."

Director of photography Dariusz Wolski, who shot all three *Pirates of the Caribbean* films with Depp, says both star and director share a less-is-more attitude to acting. "They both love silent cinema. They both love Buster Keaton, Charlie Chaplin," the Polish-born cinematographer points out. "They both love acting through gestures, looks, more than dialogue. I mean, dialogue has to be in the film, but a lot of times a look, the angle of the camera, an expression on the face is way more powerful than words."

Another direct inspiration on their Sweeney Todd was the character of Dr X, played by Lionel Atwill in 1932's *Dr X* and by none other than Humphrey Bogart in *The Return Of Dr X* seven years later. "That was so amazing, to see Humphrey Bogart playing a monster," Burton muses. "That's what I thought about Johnny playing Sweeney Todd. It's so cool to see him play a part like this. You see all those other horror movie actors do it

all the time, but [a non-horror star like] Humphrey Bogart playing Dr X, that was fantastic, so bizarre, special."

Watching Burton and Depp at work on set, it's evident they share a shorthand born out of a deep respect and understanding. "They are like any good team," says Richard Zanuck, "they have almost an unspoken way of doing things. They can practically read each other's minds. Johnny looks to Tim for guidance and Tim looks to Johnny for taking what he has outlined and pushing it a little further. So the combination is wonderful in terms of freshness and inventiveness."

And humor too. Between takes, Burton and Depp laugh constantly, sometimes uncontrollably so. "They're like Abbott and Costello," Zanuck continues. "They're like two high-school guys during recess, joking and having fun. They really love each other and would do anything for each other. It's a deep friendship, and they're both lovely people, fun to work with and hard working. And they're both at the top of their game."

Although Bonham Carter knew Depp personally through her relationship with Burton, and had acted with him briefly in *Charlie and the Chocolate Factory* – while both had provided voices for characters in *Corpse Bride* – this would be the first time that she had worked with him for any extended period of time. "He's very easy, disciplined and respectful," she says. "He's very technically aware and very helpful to everyone. And a laugh also, we had a lot of fun." She was, she admits, a little apprehensive to begin with. "Those two have a great relationship and I thought, 'Is this going to be a boys club, these two having a laugh all the time?' Their humor is pretty boyish and based on American television and American culture. A lot of the time I didn't get the references and sometimes I did feel left out: 'Tim, can you just include me a bit?' Then they did, but most of it is poo jokes!" And if her and Burton's off set relationship ever intruded on set, Depp, she says, became a good deflector. "Obviously it was tricky at times, me and Tim working together, but Johnny was a really good support and diplomat. He was a dream to work with."

For Depp, working with Burton has always been a good experience, but there was something even more special about their collaboration on *Sweeney Todd*. "He's just amazing, his vision, his drive, his passion, he's got it all," Depp relates. "My relationship with Tim, it's like family. For me, it's home. It's as simple as that. I somehow know how he works, how he ticks, and certainly, he knows me pretty much better than anyone. And we laugh at the same kind of things. I trust him beyond... He's definitely the only guy I'd go try and sing for at the ripe old age of forty-three, go into a recording studio and sing. That's for sure. He's a brother, and more than a brother."

Opposite top:
Sweeney makes his point to Mrs Lovett.

Opposite bottom:
Colleen Atwood's design for Sweeney.

Bottom:
A draining end for Sacha Baron Cohen's Pirelli.

FINDING MRS LOVETT

"Mrs Lovett is one of the great dramatic creations of 20th century theater," says screen–writer and producer John Logan. "She's a counterpoint to Sweeney, because Sweeney is very grim and brooding and very, very serious about what he's doing. Mrs Lovett brings life and energy and sort of a twinkle in her eye. Together they're an unstoppable combination."

Having wanted to play Mrs Lovett since she was a teenager, Bonham Carter was desperate to score the role in Burton's film. There was one major problem: she didn't know whether she could sing. "I've always, always wanted to be in a musical, but I never thought I could sing, except in the bathroom," she says. "But I thought, 'I have to audition. I'm not going to sit and watch Tim get involved with the most fantastic music without having a chance to get involved, because Sondheim is my

hero.' Tim understood. He said, 'I respect you as an actress but it's a singing part. You've never sung.' I said, 'Let me learn how to sing, and whether I get it or not, it'll be good for me as an actor.'"

And so Bonham Carter gave herself three months to learn to sing. "I worked my arse off," she says. "From June to September of 2006, I sang every single day and I learnt pretty much the whole score because I was very, very keen. I went to this amazing teacher called Ian Adam [who sadly passed away in 2007]. He was quite famous for making singers out of actors who can't necessarily sing. Ninety percent of what he did was give you confidence

Top:
Pining for Sweeney: "The absolute core of her is she's in love with this man who never notices her."

Bottom:
Depp and Bonham Carter with Burton on set.

and a self-belief that makes you able to open your mouth and produce a sound. I thought my only chance was to act it as well as I could. I knew Sondheim loved Judi Dench's performance in *A Little Night Music* because it was the best acted, though he conceded that she didn't have the most extraordinary voice. I thought if you go for the truth of the lyric that's my only chance."

For Burton, the idea of casting Bonham Carter as Mrs Lovett brought its own set of complications, not least because of the perception that he was giving her the part simply because she was his girlfriend. "I was very nervous about it, because it's a big role," admits Burton, who had first worked with Bonham Carter on *Planet of the Apes* and then cast her in smaller parts in *Big Fish* and *Charlie and the Chocolate Factory*. "And it wasn't just me, it was Sondheim who had to okay it. With a role like this, you've got to be able to really, really deliver."

Years before Burton had even met Bonham Carter, he had painted a quick watercolor of what he envisioned Sweeney Todd and Mrs Lovett to look like. Staring at that painting now, pinned to a notice board on the wall of his London office, it's clear they look like Depp and Bonham Carter. "I knew she looked right for it," he says. "I can see those two together. But I felt I had to really go through the process of seeing other people. I didn't want to do too many, because it's quite exposing to come in and sing."

Bonham Carter certainly wasn't the only actress who wanted the part. And so Burton flew to New York to see a number of potential Mrs Lovetts, all of whom had to sing 'The Worst Pies in London' as their audition piece. "A couple of major stars came in and 'exposed' themselves, singing the score with just a piano player, and

we videoed them," says Zanuck. "There were about eight in all. We did several in London, and there were major people who didn't come in but made their own recordings and sent them in."

Before Burton traveled to New York he had recorded Bonham Carter singing several numbers at Air Studios, London, but purposely didn't show the results to anyone, not even Zanuck. Once back in the UK, having auditioned everyone, Burton decided to eschew making a decision for a while longer. "I was extremely tortured and I left it alone for a few weeks," he admits. "Then I looked at them all, with Helena's at the end. I was perfectly expecting to say, 'I got to go with somebody else here', but I was weirdly surprised and thought, 'She's good!' Then I thought, 'How do we go through this?' because it was a bit of a political process. It wasn't with Johnny,

Top:
Mrs Lovett plays dress up.

Bottom:
Several of Colleen Atwood's designs for Mrs Lovett.

Opposite top:
Decked out in Burton's favoured black and white stripes, Todd clearly doesn't find the sea air as invigorating as Mrs Lovett.

Opposite bottom:
Sealed with a kiss: a fantasy wedding.

but it was in that particular case."

It was then that Burton showed all the tapes to Zanuck: "He put me in a projection room by myself. I played them all, and then he came in. I said, 'I don't know what to tell you but it's Helena, and I'm not saying it because of all of our relationships, I honestly believe that. Some of these people may have better voices, but this is Mrs Lovett, there's no question about it.' I must say, despite the close relationship between Tim and Helena, he was absolutely not biased. I'd never seen anyone dealing with someone that they're very close to be so objective as he was. And this wasn't a charade. We didn't put all these people through an exercise. She had less of a chance, really."

In the end, though, as with Sweeney, it was Sondheim who had final approval. The composer watched all the candidates' tapes and, without knowing Burton's choice, opted for Bonham Carter. "He said, 'I think she is far and away the best,'" Zanuck reveals. "'Not voice-wise, because there were some really skilled singers, but voice and personality and look and everything

[combined], she was Mrs Lovett.'"

Bonham Carter was, needless to say, delighted. "That's probably the best day of my life to be absolutely honest," she recalls. "I really could not believe it. I was in complete shock and Tim was too. He burst into tears. And he doesn't cry a lot."

John Logan remembers once asking Angela Lansbury who she thought should play Mrs Lovett in the movie. Her reply? Helena Bonham Carter. "She is an absolute gem in this part," he says. "Mrs Lovett is very challenging for actresses because

Helena that works for Mrs Lovett."

"I saw her as totally amoral, full of zest and full of life, and a survivor, somebody who was as zestful and vital as Sweeney was depressive and introverted. She's very canny, and a wannabe middle-class person," reveals Bonham Carter. "But the main thing that motors her, the main thing that defines Mrs Lovett is that she's tragically in love with somebody who doesn't love her back."

"I think that once Mrs Lovett and Sweeney kind of get together, his focus

the temptation is to overact the part. Her songs, 'By the Sea' and 'The Worst Pies in London' tend to be very upbeat, very bouncy. I've seen actresses on stage who have played to the back balcony, which, in a movie, would be disastrous. We were interested always in the human connection between Mrs Lovett and Sweeney Todd, knowing full well the movie rises or falls on that relationship. And Helena, because of that magnificently expressive face, is able to suggest very clearly her yearning, her suffering, while not losing – and this is really important – the twinkle in her eye. There's something very mischievous about

becomes a little clearer," says Depp. "I think she'd rather he didn't think about killing so much and maybe rather he were slightly more romantic and paid more attention to her. Eye contact is not one of his strong points, Sweeney, even with Mrs Lovett, bless her."

"There's something very sad and haunting and emotional and delusional about that kind of a character," says Burton of Mrs Lovett. "That's why they make such a perfect couple, really. It's a relationship movie. You put them next to each other and they make a weird couple and that, again, was part of the energy of it."

Above and opposite: "I saw her as totally amoral, full of zest and full of life, and a survivor," says Bonham Carter of Mrs Lovett.

FINDING THE LOOK

"It's a weird thing to say but I can see them being in a wax museum, I can see them at the London Dungeon as an exhibit," says Tim Burton of Sweeney and Mrs Lovett. "It was important just visually that they looked right for each other, that sort of perverted alliance. There's a sort of decayed, pale look to them."

"They're like creatures of the night," offers cinematographer Dariusz Wolski. "We shot a lot of tests too see how dark we can make the shadows under their eyes. What's important about Johnny's character, when he comes back to England, is that he's kind of hiding himself. He

doesn't want to be recognized as Benjamin Baker, so he plays a lot scenes with his eyes down. Most of the time his eyes are in shadow, until it's really important, until he decides to kill somebody, until there's a very emotional moment. Then he reacts and brings up his eyes so we can see them. That's part of the design of the film. It's also part of Johnny's character that you never talk about directly, but then, after a few rehearsals, you begin to understand what he's trying to convey, and you try to participate, lighting-wise, with the whole thing."

"I had started making these little draw-

ings for the character," Depp recalls, "and I started thinking, 'What should this guy look like?' I wanted his eyes to be almost recessed, surrounded by dark, trying to think of that classic horror look."

Burton wanted both Sweeney Todd and Mrs Lovett to look like silent movie stars. Both have a deathly pallor and red-rimmed eyes surrounded by pools of darkness. "We've got very, very pale skin and rather dark, sunken eyes, a bit like how Tim looks, his usual sort of aesthetic," laughs Bonham Carter whose Mrs Lovett, at times, resembles a cross between silent movie actress Lillian Gish and Bette Davis in *Whatever Happened To Baby Jane?* "He loves pale skin, dark, sunken eyes, because he's an insomniac. I think that's where it comes from. There's a lot of autobiography in there, even if it's completely unconscious.

He's so *not* a narcissist, but it always ends up being somehow a version of himself. Though he'll hate me saying that!"

Responsible for Depp and Bonham Carter's onscreen transformation was Oscar®-winning hair & makeup supervisor Peter Owen, whose credits include the *Lord of the Rings* trilogy. "Tim only gave me one real note, but with Tim that's all you need," says Owen, who worked with Burton on *Charlie and the Chocolate Factory* and *Sleepy Hollow* and with Depp on *Sleepy Hollow* and *The Libertine*. "He just said silent film-style horror movie. And I thought, 'Yeah, if I put that together with some music and Tim Burton, I know the world we're in.' Immediately you forget you're doing a period movie, which, to begin with, I had to keep reminding all our assistants, no, we're not doing a period movie. There's

an orchestra playing and Tim Burton is directing. If something looks right, it's right. It doesn't matter whether it's accurate to any period."

For Mrs Lovett, Owen followed Burton's desire for her to have "particularly deranged hair" while for Sweeney he not only darkened Depp's own brown locks but added a greenish tinge that would work with the color

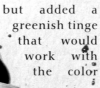

desaturation process planned for post-production, as well as a small hair piece with a white streak that brings to mind not only *Bride of Frankenstein* but also *Dr X*.

"When we were messing around doing the early camera tests," Depp reveals. "I was almost thinking about doing like a shock of white, white hair, but thought that would be too much. Then Peter Owen said, 'I made you this white wig but I also made you this kind of white shock, this skunk's thing,' and I thought, 'Oh yeah, let's have a look at that.' Chucked it on, and there it was. The puzzle was complete."

As for Sweeney's clothes, costume designer Colleen Atwood opted for a plain, austere look. "It's a very simple character. He basically has two different looks except for in Mrs Lovett's fantasy numbers," she explains. Atwood had Sweeney's long leather

Opposite:
The flamboyant
Pirelli looks down on
Sweeney.

Left:
Two of Colleen Atwood's
designs for Adolfo Pirelli.

Sweeney Todd

SWEENEY TODD

This spread:
Collage depicting images that
inspired the costume designs
for Sweeney Todd, along with

overcoat manufactured by a firm in Italy then cut into it with a laser to give it the texture of stripes, while for his waistcoats she took an antique bed sheet that was then dyed, distressed and cut into shape.

"One thing that came a bit later was the kind of holster rig for his razors," she continues. "We were trying to figure out how we could make a pocket in his work jacket to put the razors in. Then the idea

came up to have a holster so we made this holster with hobnails in. And then I put hobnails on his boots. We had fun with these little details that may or may not be seen on screen, but the ideas were fun to evolve with Johnny."

"These blades are his family," explains Depp of the cutthroat razors that Sweeney sings to in 'My Friends'. "They're an extension of him, but they're the only loves in his life now that his family's gone."

"I always thought of Sweeney's razor like King Arthur's Excalibur," says Logan. "It was something that gave him strength, gave him comfort, gave him power. He's been denied his razor for fifteen years. So when he returns to London, Mrs Lovett gives him a box. He opens it and it's his razors. It's a connection to his past, a connection to Lucy, his dead wife, a connection to everything that's important in his life. And when Johnny picks up the first razor and holds it, it is one of the most breathtaking moments you will ever see. It is a pure moment of love."

Opposite top:
Costume designer Colleen
Atwood at work.

Opposite
bottom:
Costume designs for characters at the masked ball.

Left:
Costume designs for Mrs
Lovett and Toby.

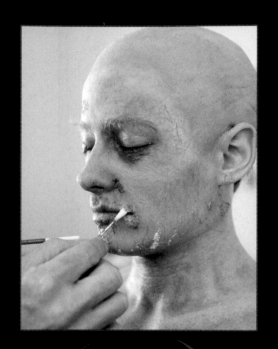

Opposite:
Laura Michelle Kelly is
transformed into the Beggar
Woman.

This page:
Helena Bonham Carter finally
gets her Mrs Lovett hairdo.

FINDING A SUPPORTING CAST

As the object of Sweeney Todd's monomaniacal vengeance, Judge Turpin needed to be played by actor of serious stature. "It is a pivotal role," says Richard Zanuck. "He's the reason for Sweeney being sent off to prison and when he lands back in London this is the one guy he wants to get. Obviously we needed someone who would be an equal opponent of Johnny. He had to sing. He had to be very nasty. And nobody can be meaner, with doing very little, just his look, than Alan Rickman. He also has a wonderful voice."

Although singing was part of Rickman's training at London's Royal Academy of Dramatic Arts (RADA), the actor had never sung on film before. "I did play the male lead in the end of year musical and, early days in rep, I was in the chorus of *Guys and Dolls*," he reveals. "I'd always enjoyed singing, but never thought anything like this would come along. It's quite good to meet those Waterloos when you least expect it."

For Pirelli, the flamboyant barber who rumbles Barker/Sweeney's new identity but who turns out to have a secret of his own, Burton cast talented British comic actor Sacha Baron Cohen, in his first film since his breakout success with *Borat: Cultural Leanings of America Make for Benefit Glorious Nation of Kazakhstan*.

"We got him before we saw *Borat*, and before he became a household name," explains Zanuck. "He asked to come in. It

wasn't our idea. We met him for the first time in a recording studio. Didn't realize how tall he is, about six-five or six-six, and very handsome, actually. He told us he's always loved this show, and that he had sung early on in his life in choirs, so we asked him to step into the booth. He hadn't prepared to sing from *Sweeney Todd*, but he sang practically all of *Fiddler on the Roof*. And he did it in such a way that Tim and I were literally on the floor, buckled over. He was so funny, but despite all the laughter we realized this guy's got a great voice. He had the part right then and there as far as we were concerned. And he's wonderful. Sacha is extraordinary in the picture."

"It's a schizophrenic part," notes John Logan. "On one hand Pirelli has the most entertaining song in the show, 'The Contest', where, literally, he is putting on a show for the people of St Dunstan's Market and he has a challenge with Sweeney. Then he has a completely private scene with Todd where that mask comes off and the jovial Italianate persona that he's projecting completely disappears to be replaced by a ruthless ice-cold blackmailer. There's not a bigger transition in the movie. You will laugh out loud at the inventiveness of selling that song to an audience, but then, when he's not playing the character Pirelli, he is so ice cold and so frightening that you truly realize what a gifted actor he is."

Playing Judge Turpin's nefarious henchman Beadle Bamford is Timothy Spall, one of Britain's most respected film, TV and stage actors and a veteran of several Mike Leigh films, as well as the *Harry Potter* series in which he plays Peter Pettigrew. Like Rickman, Spall graduated from RADA and had sung there, as well as in Mike Leigh's Gilbert & Sullivan musical comedy *Topsy-Turvy*.

"My character, he's a nasty piece of work really," says Spall. "He's a small-time parish official who has adopted authority because of his association with the Judge, who he's ingratiated himself with in many ways. He's sort of his bodyguard, his henchman.

He's a procurer of various things, seemly and unseemly. Also, he's pretty violent. He's not very nice!"

Rounding out the rest of the cast were a coterie of talented newcomers, all making their feature film débuts: sixth form student Jamie Campbell Bower (Anthony), Jayne Wisener (Johanna), who's in her second year

at the Royal Academy of Music and Drama in Glasgow, and schoolboy Ed Saunders (Toby), as well as Laura Michelle Kelly, a veteran of London's West End whose theatrical credits include the musicals *Mamma Mia*, *Mary Poppins* and *Lord of the Rings*, who plays the dual roles of Sweeney's wife Lucy and the Beggar Woman.

Opposite:
Tim Burton asks Ed Saunders'
Toby for some hair advice.

Left:
Toby unveils the latest
papal look.

Next spread:
Pirelli – clearly a man not
afraid to under sell himself.

MAKING MUSIC

The time-honored way of filming a movie musical is to record the songs in advance, and then have the actors lip-synch to the playback on set.

"The music is so important," says Richard Zanuck. "The story is being told through the singing. We were determined that every cast member would use their own voice."

But apart from Laura Michelle Kelly, not one of the *Sweeney Todd* cast was a professional singer. Even more challenging was the fact that these first-timers had to sing Sondheim compositions.

"Stephen Sondheim writes the most complicated music in the history of the musical theater," says John Logan. "For these performers, it's like a mountain climber climbing Mount

Everest without oxygen and without Sherpas. Stephen Sondheim, particularly *Sweeney Todd*, is like singing *Don Giovanni*. It's like singing Mozart. These actors had to take a score which is so complicated it looks like geometry, and master it."

"The greatness of Sondheim, and I do think he is kissed by it," says Alan Rickman, "is that he has the lyrics in his mind, he's got the character in his mind, he's got the music in his mind, and you've got to match all of them. But they're all there if you work at it and listen to it and hand yourself over to it. It's a bit like Shakespeare. If you look at a piece of Shakespeare, it tells you how to say it, if you obey the punctuation. And breathe. Great writing's done it for you. Stop thinking you're better than it – it's doing the work. Match it."

"Sondheim melodies are really tough," agrees Johnny Depp. "Certain things felt very natural because they're beautiful melodies, so if you had familiarized yourself with them as much as I had, they were locked in to the degree that you could kind of deviate slightly. It's Stephen Sondheim, so you wouldn't want to deviate in terms of melody, you sing the notes, but you can mess around with the timing a little bit. For example, 'My Friends' felt pretty natural and not as difficult as, say, 'Epiphany'. That's a real booger. There are a lot of half steps; whole steps are easier to sing than half steps, I don't know why, at least for me. So it's super-challenging, no question about that."

But before a song could be sung or a note recorded, it fell to music supervisor Mike Higham to dissect the songs line-by-line, verse-by-verse. "Tim gave me a very early version of the script and had me go through it and look at the structure of the songs, how long they were, was there anything repeated in the songs that was repeated in the dialogue after, to see whether there was a flow in the music, and make sure it didn't feel too repetitive or too long," reveals Higham, who'd previously worked with Burton on the music for *Corpse Bride*.

Then, using a recording of the original Broadway production starring Angela Lansbury, Higham edited together a version of each song to work out how long each number could and should be. "There were some songs that got dropped out of the script, but Tim still liked sections of them," Higham reveals, "so I musically lifted some of those to put them into the same incarnations of other songs. We tried to mix and match to get the best of everything."

To give the actors something to rehearse with, Higham created a version of the score without singing, a backing track effectively.

Listening to the music, without the vocal melody, was, according to Depp, something of a revelation. "To be able to hear the various layers, the string section, the horns, to hear them almost isolated was a real eye-opener," he says. "I didn't realize it was that complicated.

Even when I saw it on stage, it didn't seem that complicated to me. But you hear it without the vocals and there are these really incredibly dissonant chords, these notes that pass by each other, that, when you hear the whole piece, you don't really pay that much attention to. When it's all isolated you hear these dissonant things happening. Why did he do that? *How* did he do that? Then you come to the conclusion that he's got to be certifiably insane," Depp laughs. "Anybody who can write that kind of stuff has got to be just nuts, really. To decide that we're going to go from 7/8 to 3/4, from this weird time signature to, suddenly, a waltz, and while all that's going on, the glockenspiel's doing this and the cellos are doing that. What? Doesn't make sense."

"It's potentially a complete cacophony," agrees Helena Bonham Carter, "but when the harmonies happen, they're so beautiful because it sounds so unlikely. But what I love is there's always an emotional sense. I've got 'Wait' which is a lovely lullaby, which seems rather simple, but underneath it's horrible. The piano sounds so disturbed. But that, of course, is Sweeney's state of mind. So a lot of themes and the unease and the fact it never resolves itself is a reflection of the mind and the heart and the emotional landscape of Sweeney."

It was to those early backing tracks that Tim Burton first heard what Bonham Carter and Depp, who recorded ninety percent of his songs to Higham's mock-up in Los Angeles, sounded like together. "There was a magical moment when he sent back 'A Little Priest'," Higham recalls. "Helena sang her part in the studio and we put them together in the computer. And, bingo, there it was. That was

the first time Tim had ever heard the two of them sing together. It was the first time Stephen had ever heard the two of them sing. We all just sat back and laughed. It was like, 'Wow, this is fantastic.' It worked."

Adapting the *Sweeney Todd* score from its stage origins to a movie required a much larger orchestra than permissible in the theater, with sixty-four musicians drafted in to play the score at the recording sessions, the largest number ever to have performed it. "When you listen to any of the Broadway recordings the orchestra's not that big," explains Higham. "Maybe thirty, forty people, because, of course, in theater, you don't have the space and you've got to cram everybody in the pit. But the moment you want it on a big screen, you want to have it bigger. We added thirty violins, some more horns, a tuba, just to give a big, fatter, wider sound. Tim likes simple melodies and darkness, and when you take the melodies away from some of the songs, the underscoring between dialogue, it's very simple, it's very dark, and having extra strings makes it feel wide and it sort of glues to the picture a bit better. This is definitely its own unique thing."

The score was recorded during a four-day period at Air Studios, London with the bespoke orchestra overseen by Stephen Sondheim and conducted by his musical supervisor Paul Gemignani.

"That was a fascinating experience for all of us to sit there with Tim on one side and Stephen Sondheim on the other," remembers producer Richard Zanuck. "This was his arena because he can hear a flute that's slightly off, like Tim can see out of the corner of his eye an extra a hundred yards away down the street. It was a wonderful experience, hearing the orchestra with perfect sound."

Unlike conventional film scoring sessions, where the music is recorded to a finished cut of the film, with *Sweeney Todd* Higham was faced with the incredibly complicated task of laying down the entire score without a picture to work to, and therefore having to predict what would be shot months later by Burton on set. "In the script, there are lots of moments where songs come out of singing, go into dialogue with underscore, which is still part of the song, and come back into singing," he explains. "With things like that, it was very difficult to gauge, not knowing the pace of how the dialogue would be spoken."

In a number of cases, Higham was forced to second-guess when and where an instrumental section would be needed. "I tried to allow for much longer time, because it's much easier to lift something out than put it back in," he notes. "We always tried to keep the vocals separate from the orchestra, so we'd have the backing track only, if we wanted to work with that on set. There were several times in the studio where I'd ask Tim, 'Do you think that's long enough? How long do you think Mrs Lovett's going to take to walk down that flight of stairs?' And he would be like, 'I have no idea!' So that was a challenge. Have we got enough? Have we

got too little? Is it the right dynamic? So we'd do multiple versions, just in case."

Once the score was recorded, the songs were next. But before any of the voice tracks could be laid down, all the cast got the opportunity to rehearse for Sondheim.

"That was really nerve wracking," says Bonham Carter. "I'd been cast by him, then I had to sing for him. And he was going to give us his notes. But thankfully he was fine."

"I can sing, but I'm not a singer, put it that way," notes Timothy Spall. "I have sung before and seemed to have got away with it. Stephen

Sondheim has a huge reputation as a brilliant composer and lyricist. To have to sing in front of him was a bit like doing Hamlet in front of Shakespeare, really."

Rickman describes the experience as one of life's more challenging moments. "You've got the music in your hand and Stephen Sondheim walks across the room and says, 'Okay, let's hear it,'" he recalls. "It doesn't get much tougher than that. Watching him watching us was an extraordinary experience. There was one day where we were all singing 'The Ballad of Sweeney Todd', and he was like somebody tied up with concentration. He wasn't watching because his eyes were so shut. He's inside this thing he's made."

As well as advising the cast on their singing, Bonham Carter says Sondheim had very firm ideas on how they should interpret their characters, which, in her case, didn't always coincide with what she had in mind.

"I wanted her to be sexual and sensual and not older than Sweeney," she says of Mrs Lovett. "I think Sondheim always saw her as older than him and a sort of maternal figure. I wanted her to have a side that was a bit of a slut, frankly. I even thought, maybe she makes her living by being a prostitute, which was pretty common in Victorian times, but Sondheim didn't like the idea at all." Still, the composer's most useful character note to her was, she says, to think of Stella Dallas from *A Streetcar Named Desire*. "Because she's a common middle-class wannabe. Singing-wise he didn't give me many notes, he was refreshingly un-controlling, actually. But he's very precise about his details. On 'Worst Pies' he said don't flirt; that was the prostitute conversation. So it was more acting, not much with the singing."

There is, however, a huge difference bet-ween performing in the theater, having to fill an auditorium with your voice, and singing on film. Not only does cinema's close-ups of the actors mean a less stagy, more intimate style of acting, but the fact one's voice doesn't have to project to the back balcony means the cast could sing more quietly, as opposed to "standing on the front of the stage, yelling," says Rickman. "If you're in a small room, why would you be singing loudly? It's the first time, I think, that a Sondheim musical has been filmed, so you get to hear the complexities of the music."

Vocal recording took place over six weeks at both Air Studios and Eden Studios, London under the supervision of Higham. Out of the cast, it was Bonham Carter who had the most songs. "And the hardest stuff to sing," says Higham. "Helena's a complete blast. She's a real trouper. Just keep feeding her coffee, Diet Coke, fresh juices, you name it, and she'll get there in the end. And she gave us plenty of options. Some songs she sang 30 times, others five times. And Ed Sanders, who plays Toby, he was fantastic too. He nearly made Tim cry when he sang 'Not While I'm Around', which is the big ballad that he sings with Helena. He's a thirteen year-old kid and he just nailed the song. It's beautiful. He was an absolute joy."

Sacha Baron Cohen had two songs as Pirelli. "Sacha took it very seriously," recalls Higham, "and we spent a very late evening working with a soprano teacher because Sacha wanted to know how you do real vibrato, like an Italian opera singer. At the end of one number, he has to hit this huge high G. Tim thought that was hilarious and wanted him to continue it, and continue it, as if he had lungs of a giant."

Although the *Sweeney Todd* score features several duets, including numbers between Sweeney and Mrs Lovett, Sweeney and Anthony, Sweeney and Judge Turpin, and Mrs Lovett and Toby, none were actually recorded as duets, with everyone singing their parts separately. Rickman, who sings 'Pretty Women' with Sweeney, suggested that Depp record his section first so that he knew what to feed himself into, particularly as his voice is much lower than Depp's. "I said I'd better listen to him, and when I did I thought, 'Oh ****, this is a *proper* singer," he laughs. "I mean, people who don't know are going to be amazed. And then they're going to be wondering when his album's coming out."

Previous spread:
Sondheim's musical supervisor Paul Gemignani conducts the "Sweeney Todd" orchestra at Air Studios, London.

Opposite:
Burton and music supervisor Mike Higham.

Unlike most musicals, the story of *Sweeney Todd* is told predominantly through music and lyrics rather than dialogue, meaning the recording sessions became more than just

about getting the songs musically correct. Because the actors would be singing on set to their pre-recorded tracks, they were forced to find their performance in the recording booth and commit to it there and then, rather than later during principal photography.

"It's a very different discipline," says Depp. "On the one hand it eliminates certain pressures, certain responsibilities – spontaneity, the birth of a moment, allowing yourself to react to things that are just happening. In this case the moment had been created in the studio. The second you laid down the song you made your choices, you've committed months in advance. At the same time, you've got to match yourself to it [on set], but make it bigger, make it better, with the visuals. Fifty percent of the work is done but the visual adds so much more. Actually, I was a lot less freaked out by it than I thought I was going to be."

During Mrs Lovett's signature song 'The Worst Pies in London', Bonham Carter's character not only has to sing but make an entire pie from scratch, including rolling the pastry, adding the meat filling, and making a

simple decoration. "It's a brilliant song. Very complicated. It's incredibly fast and really brilliant at setting up her character because it captures her as somebody who just goes off at tangents, is all over the place, somewhat frenetic, but, equally, gets over the fact that she's running a pie shop. So it's quite hard work."

In addition to learning the song forwards, backwards and sideways – "I think I've sung it probably nearing 500 times, from when I started singing and auditioning, and then recording it, and the different choices. I could do it sleep walking now" – Bonham Carter took lessons in pie making from Katherine Tidy, a period pie maker and home economist. "I made a few pies so at least I understood the whole chemistry of making a pie," she explains, "shortcrust pastry, the meat, what kind of pies they were. We had lots of decisions to make, actually. And then blocking it. Ideally I wanted it to be a bit like *Blue Peter* [the legendary British children's TV show which often features cookery demonstrations] crossed with Nigella Lawson. Somehow Mrs Lovett makes a pie, but it's in front of your eyes, in the cloud of chaos. While she's non-stop chattering she produces a pie at the end. And it's not that long a song. The physicality and relationship to everything is vital when you're acting. It was hard work. In film you have to do everything exactly the same because of continuity, every single thing on the same lyric. I'm quite good at multi-tasking, but 'Worst Pies' is like the Olympics of multi-tasking."

Not that that song was the only one to cause Bonham Carter trouble. "'By the Sea' is really tricky because there's no space to breathe at all," she explains. "I was comforted to read that Angela Lansbury had said she actually confronted Sondheim and said, 'Well, where do I breathe?' And he said, 'I didn't write anywhere you could breathe. You just don't.' You have to be really fit."

"It is about breath," agrees Rickman, "if you have enough breath in your body for Sondheim. And he is a killer from that point of view. He doesn't indicate to you where to breathe at all."

For Depp, having to sustain certain notes for up to twelve beats wasn't easy. "There were several instances when I thought, I'm going to hit the deck," he remembers. "I ran out of air about five minutes ago and I might just pass out. But somehow I stayed upright. I don't know how but I did. But it's beautiful stuff to sing. I can only imagine that it must be really nice if you're a singer. But as an actor, as a kind of novice, desperately trying to do the right thing, to do it justice, was not easy."

While Bonham Carter has the most songs, she contends that it's the men who have the more beautiful, more romantic numbers. "They've got all the pretty ones," she laughs. "I've got the complicated ones." Her favorite of her songs is 'A Little Priest'. "Because it's the first time that Sweeney actually listens to her. He's in his own world, and I'm trying to get in there, but he's locked me out. Suddenly he hears me because I come up with this fantastic brainwave of popping the body into pies. It's so romantic. There's a sort of waltz theme that then recurs throughout the film, and it's so beautiful and fun. And the lyrics are brilliant. Having said that, it was one of the trickiest things to film because there are a lot of linguistic jokes, and it's pretty difficult to play without seeming arch or 'Isn't this funny?'"

Principal photography began on February 5, 2007 and was scheduled to last until April 27, although filming ran through to mid-May when Depp's young daughter fell ill, and the production closed down for two weeks in

order for him to be with her.

On set, there would be virtually no live singing. Instead, the cast was required to lip-synch to playback of their songs. Due to the complexity of Sondheim's lead ins, however, each song was given a number of "click tracks" which would indicate to the actors when to start singing.

"Lip-synching is tricky, because you've got to act it as if it's new and yet you are obeying something you've done in the past," observes Bonham Carter. "Don't look as if you're remembering or illustrating or demonstrating something. You've got to be in the moment or try and do something to keep it alive. In some ways I thought I wanted to do it live. The sound wouldn't be as good, but at least then you're free to do whatever and see what happens in the moment. Also it's quite difficult to sing internally because it's a physical act singing,

that's why people look funny when they sing because you have to contort your body into funny shapes to produce the sound."

"I didn't find lip-synching all that difficult," says Depp. "If you have rhythm and you've listened to the stuff, then it'll fall into place pretty naturally, especially if you were in the right place when you sang it. Again, I thought it was going to freak me out, but it turned out to be some of the most fun."

And if Depp did mess up on set, he at least had the security of his friend Bruce Witkin there to watch out for any missed cues, misplaced words or fluffed lines, with Higham charged with keeping an eye on Bonham Carter and the other singing cast members.

The key to successful lip-synching, reveals Higham, is to try and make sure you're really singing. "One of the things that makes it look good, is that you can see their muscles moving," he says. "You can tell people aren't singing if they don't do it. So I had to stand very close to the camera and remind people, 'That word was a bit late', because there's only a certain amount you can do in post." In addition to his lip-synching duties, Higham was always on set to administer any last-minute musical changes made by Burton. "If he thinks, 'This song needs four bars taking out', then I can lift that out of the playback, because we've got a full computer system on set, so we can practically do almost anything," Higham explains. "We can transpose things. We can slow things down, speed things up. So if Tim suddenly feels like one part needs to be slower, I can do that."

Often, between takes, Bonham Carter could be found in the back of a car or in her trailer listening to her songs on an iPod. "The big thing I learnt on this is muscle memory," she says. "If you do something vocally, or listen to something enough times your brain and your body will compute it so you don't have to think about it. So if you listen to it a few times before the take you'll know it, your body will know it, you don't have to think intellectually, you'll just do it. There were times Mike would say, 'You're late', and I didn't think I was. But you're oblivious to the fact you're a second late. That's why I practiced and I practiced and I practiced."

As the production's only professional singer, Laura Michelle Kelly couldn't believe how good Depp and Bonham Carter were at singing. "I wouldn't have imagined that it's the first time they've had to sing in public view," she says. "Everyone's so confident. It helps to be able to express a lyric as opposed to singing it with no meaning, and they've taken to it like ducks to water. Most people find Sondheim the hardest thing to sing, what with the tempos and the changes and the lyrical melodies; all of them are difficult. Watching Helena and Johnny, I'm amazed. Some people try for years to do what they're doing naturally. I'm learning lots watching them."

Despite the complexity of the musical numbers and the lip-synching involved, Burton chose not to rehearse his cast in advance of filming, preferring the spontaneity that comes with staging each sequence on the day of shooting. For the performers involved in duets, that meant the first time they would get to sing together would be on set. Rickman recalls filming his 'Pretty Women' duet with Depp as being something of a logistical challenge, with his character, Judge Turpin, sitting in Sweeney's barber's chair, being shaved by Todd, who is standing behind him. "Can't look at him because he's behind. Haven't sung with him, so you haven't heard the two of you singing together. Plus you've got your face covered with shaving cream. He's got to work out how not to get it in my mouth, and you have to work out, technically, how to stretch your lips because it's not going to be great if you've got shaving foam going in on your teeth. So there are a whole bundle of things to think about. And then lip-synching."

The only person to actually sing live on set was Laura Michelle Kelly as the Beggar Woman. "Because of the nature of her character, she's weird and needed to sort of sing, speak, sing, speak, so many times she comes out of

also opened up a new world of possibilities in terms of filming. "The prerecording kind of gave it a rhythm and I think Johnny really enjoyed that aspect of it," he says. "You felt like you could channel Lon Chaney or something. There was something very interesting about moving to music. It's interesting that it helps everybody, it puts everybody in the right zone."

Although *Sweeney Todd: The Demon Barber of Fleet Street* could never be described as being

"Sometimes a story or stage production has to wait a long time until the right people come together to turn it into a motion picture. That's what has happened with *Sweeney Todd* and I'm excited as well as confident it will be a first-rate and startling movie."

– STEPHEN SONDHEIM

dialogue and goes into song, it needed to be so of the moment. Tim took the choice to let her do that live," reveals Higham. There were several challenges associated with that, notably being able to record her vocals clearly, but, in the end says Higham, it was felt the challenges would be far outweighed by the performance, "because you'll really feel that she's there".

And yet recording all the songs live would have been impossible, not just because of the huge technical problems that would have been involved, but also the enormous cost of having an orchestra on set every day for ten weeks. "And we need the control," Higham explains. "People need the time and the quietness to be in the studio to make peace with the song. They need to be able to really make it their own. I wanted everybody to learn the songs so well that they can forget about singing and they can carry on acting, because if you've got to think, 'I've got to sing, I've got to act, I've got to move', it's a lot to think about. Concentrate on one thing at a time. So if they've got the song in the can, and it's recorded, that's one less thing they've got to think about. And we've got the optimum control in the recording studio."

Burton found having music on set, in the form of the playback, not only lent the production the air of being a silent movie but

a mainstream musical in the vein of *Chicago*, *The Producers*, *Hairspray*, or even *Dreamgirls*, to name four razzmatazz stage shows that have been turned into films in recent years, Burton was determined to remove any and all remnants of the production's Broadway roots from his version.

"Even though the music is right out of the show, it's been desaturated of the usual Broadway gloss," says Richard Zanuck. "And even though you'll hear bigger orchestrations, when Tim's through with them, those orchestrations will be even more in keeping with people singing to one another in a room. The tone is the same, the emotions are the same, but it's not actors breaking into song. There's more music in this than there is dialogue, but it's not the kind of music that you normally hear."

"On Broadway you're sitting in an audience and a song ends with a ta-da, cue for applause. You don't want to do that in a movie," explains Burton. "But you also want it to build up to what it's supposed to build to. On one level you say you're doing a silent movie so there's certain amount of acting style which you might say is a bit broad, but at the same time you try and cut out completely any Broadway kind of singing, although there's a couple of moments. So it was a weird dynamic to find. Being broad

like you might be in a silent movie or an old horror movie without being too Broadway."

"There were times when you felt you were making a silent movie," agrees Depp. "Because of the music and because of the songs, you were able to kind of be slightly more expressive, so you arrive at a place that almost teeters on German Expressionism, that kind of *Cabinet of Dr Caligari* thing."

"Tim wants everything to be internalized," concurs Bonham Carter. "He's got a real barometer for over-the-topness, and he asked me, although I'm an extrovert, to bring everything back, hardly ever use my hands, which I found quite hard. He said, 'No, no, looks theatrical.' Don't use my eyebrows too, which tend to be hyperactive anyway, try and keep it as still as possible, which is quite difficult with me because I'm quite mobile. With the songs and my accent, I could have been really broad. He said because you're singing and in a big environment, you've

got to counteract that with a very restrained performance. He wants supernaturalism."

"I think the most important thing that Tim is bringing to this world beyond his aesthetic sensibility is his entertainment sensibility," says Logan. "This is not a recording of a Broadway show, this is not a flat presentation of a piece of theater that people have loved for twenty years, this is a movie. This is our Sweeney Todd. Tim has been hyper-conscious of anything that smacks of too emotive, too presentation, too "cute" in terms of the actors over performing or playing to the back balcony. Tim has been wonderful about keeping it real, keeping it honest, and making sure these are real people going through this terribly difficult story and not shying away from the really harrowing emotions. As a theater fan and a movie fan I think he's doing the perfect thing, saying, 'We respect the stage play, we love the stage play, but this has to be first and foremost a work of cinema.'"

Above:
"It goes something like this..." Tim Burton taps out the right rhythm.

85

Above:
A concept sketch of
Sweeney's ship approaching
Tower Bridge by production
designer Dante Ferretti.

*Opposite
top:*
Dante Ferretti in his
Pinewood Studios office.

*Opposite
bottom:*
A Dante Ferretti concept
drawing of a London street.

The man responsible for bringing Burton's vision of 19th century London to life is two-time Oscar®-winning production designer Dante Ferretti. A quiet, unassuming Italian with broken English, Ferretti is one of the all-time greats, having worked with the late Italian filmmaker Federico Fellini on six films, as well as Martin Scorsese on *The Age of Innocence, Gangs of New York, Casino, Kundun* and *The Aviator*, Brian De Palma on *The Black Dahlia*, and Neil Jordan on *Interview With the Vampire*. Prior to *Sweeney Todd* Ferretti had been working with Burton on another project, *Ripley's Believe It or Not!*,

a biopic of oddity collector Robert Ripley that was due to star Jim Carrey, before being postponed.

Burton first met Ferretti in a restaurant in Rome some years ago. "He was with a friend of mine," recalls Ferretti, "and he said, 'We have to work together some day because I love Fellini and I love your work.' I always thought Tim remind me of Fellini, because he is so creative, he always make a little sketch, exactly like him. Also Fellini, he makes many caricatures, so they are very close to each other."

"I've seen Dante's work since the Fellini

days and there's just an energy about working with somebody who's worked with Fellini," enthuses Burton, who also shares Fellini's fondness for berets. "It roots you in the fact you're making a movie and not in a business. He's an artist. You walk by his room and he does his own drawings. There's some real energy to that, and the history and all the stuff he's done, that was exciting to me."

Burton wasn't interested in Ferretti creating an historically accurate recreation of 19th century London for *Sweeney Todd* and sent the Rome-based designer a DVD of Rowland V. Lee's 1939 *Son of Frankenstein*, the third in the Universal horror movie series, as a guide to the look he was after. "He said I want to do London that's a little bit like an old black and white Hollywood movie," Ferretti reveals. "Not too many details, it has to be like black and white in color, just a few colors, don't put too many colors, it will be desaturated in the post-production." A few days later the two men met in London to discuss the project. Ferretti arrived armed with sketches for Fleet Street, Sweeney's Barber Shop, Mrs Lovett's bakehouse and

Judge Turpin's ballroom, one of a handful of sets that would have any color in them: that color being red.

The approach Burton and Ferretti ultimately opted for was a slightly more fantasy image of London, rather than setting it in a specific time period.

"We decided not to be real hardcore because it is kind of a fable and it's slightly stylized," Burton notes. "It's like those *Frankenstein* movies, they didn't go: 'The Romanian mountains 1740'. By not doing that, there's a certain amount of fable aspect that feels important to the piece. This one

you want to keep in that fantasy London world. I didn't want to get too late, because the story starts into the time when Jack the Ripper was around, and I wanted it to feel a bit earlier than that, just a slightly earlier, slightly cruder time, without acknowledging it."

And so the movie opens with a shot of Sweeney arriving in London, traveling along the River Thames by ship and passing under an under-construction Tower Bridge, even though the world famous London landmark wasn't actually built when the movie's ostensibly set. Although in a concession to history, the bridge in the film isn't the one we see today. "We lose the walkway on top," Ferretti explains, "because it's very powerful these two towers, without the other bridge on top."

While Burton is renowned for creating amazing fantasy worlds by traditional filmmaking techniques – namely building sets on soundstages and studio back lots rather than using CGI – he had initially planned to shoot *Sweeney Todd* in the manner of *Sin City*, using minimal sets and props and filming his actors against green screens, with everything else computer-generated in post-production.

"Part of the reason was the budget," he explains. "But when I really thought about it, being on a set helps me, it helps the

Top:
A model of London's Old Bailey.

Right:
A blueprint for an Old Bailey column.

Opposite top:
Filming Alan Rickman and Timothy Spall leaving the Old Bailey in front of a green screen...

Opposite bottom:
The finished article in all its computer generated glory.

actors, it helps everybody. And at the end of the day, people are singing. And singing on a green screen, you're so far removed from any reality that it would have been a really scary nightmare. I think that made it even more important to have sets on this one because of that, because of the singing."

Producer Richard Zanuck says the cost difference between building sets and using the green screen method was minimal. "We realized that for substantially the same as doing it digitally, we could, if we did it intelligently with set extension and a little green screen, build sets," he reveals. "And Tim certainly feels much more comfortable and so do the actors. There's nothing worse, or so I've heard, than spending months and months in front of a green screen, fighting imaginary beasts."

"It gives you nothing back, it's a drain," notes Helena Bonham Carter who, nevertheless, had to film a few scenes for *Sweeney Todd* in front of a green screen and found the experience horrible. "We had to do the whole 'By the Sea' sequence in a green expanse and there's something about being suspended in the space and the green that makes you feel sick and very disembodied."

For Ferretti, the decision to build sets was a welcome one, although it clearly meant

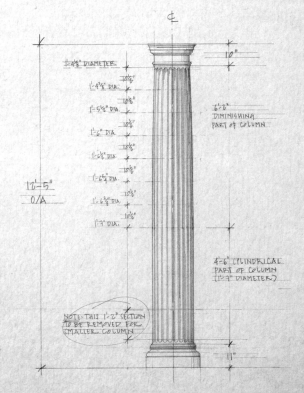

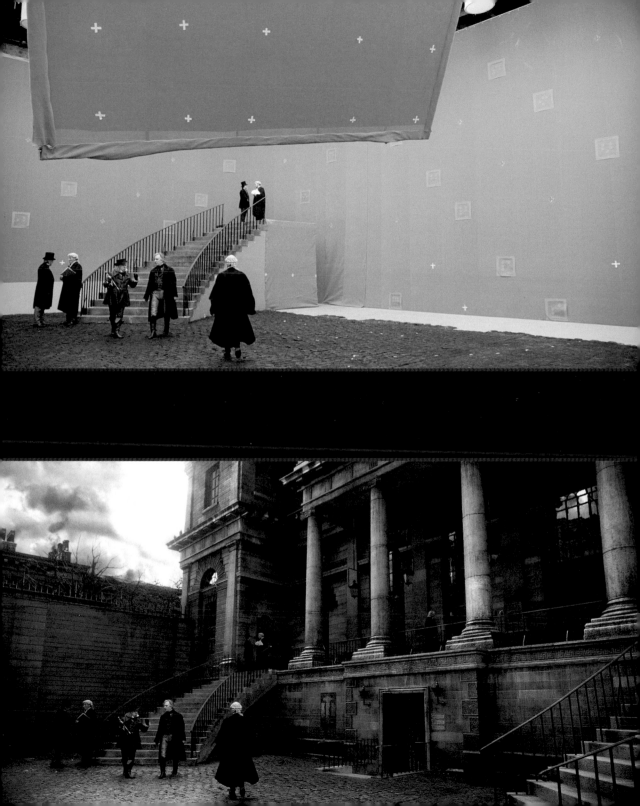

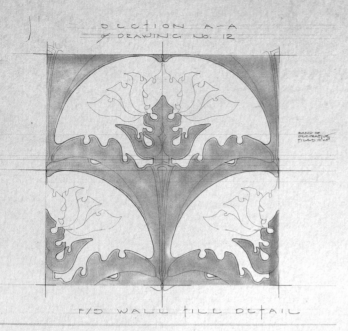

there was the relative tightness of the film's budget, which required much ingenuity on his behalf to not only create the large number of sets required by the script but also build them on the small number of available soundstages.

Ferretti's solution was simple, ingenious and remarkably cost effective: he reused his sets. The one for St Dunstan's Market, a huge street set, was built on Pinewood's S Stage, and used for a number of scenes, among them Sweeney's and Pirelli's shaving contest. By incorporating movable walls and interchangeable storefronts, Ferretti created a set that could be easily overhauled and extended, and transformed into London's Fleet Street, a set which included the interior and exterior of Mrs Lovett's Pie Shop, as well as the exterior of Sweeney's Barber Shop, the interior of which was built on R Stage, along with the bakehouse and Judge Turpin's ballroom.

"This is our first time with Dante and he's exceeded our expectations," says Zanuck. "It's extraordinary what he's done. You're going to feel like you're in London at that time period and, obviously, we have set extensions that are done digitally so you'll get the feeling it's a big, outdoor picture."

much more work upfront for him and his team. Under the green screen plan, Judge Turpin's house, for instance, was little more than a simple window and door set shot against a green screen background. Swapping to traditional sets meant the set became an entire house, complete with a tree-lined street and enormous painted backdrop.

In all, Ferretti was responsible for more than a dozen full sets at England's Pinewood Studios, where Burton had previously filmed *Batman* and *Charlie and the Chocolate Factory*. The challenges he faced were mainly twofold. Firstly, there was a shortened pre-production period. "Normally I have more weeks to think about the movie, to design the movie, to make a model, to discuss, and with this we have very small time, but I think we did pretty good." And then

While Burton's films all have a very distinct look, there is a signature style to them that makes them uniquely his. Ferretti says that *Sweeney Todd* will be slightly different. "This movie is without curves," the designer notes. "Everything is very graphic. This is the word he say in the beginning. He

say 'Dante, I like something graphic.' Not too many details, just a few things. Tim is really creative. He has a very clear idea what he wants. He's a great, great director and if you look at all his movies, the look is one of the most important things."

Walking around the *Sweeney Todd* sets,

SIDE ELEVATION

the detailing and sheer artistry involved is astonishing. Step through any storefront and you'll find a fully stocked shop inside, be it Edwin Walker Esq., purveyor of fine perfumery, or Bailey & Granger's Tobacco Store, or the butchers with numerous (fake) animals hanging from hooks.

"There's something miraculous when, as a writer, you write INT. PIE SHOP and then you see what Dante and Tim have created," says John Logan. "I know Dante very well because he did *The Aviator*, and I knew he would bring his fine love of detail to this world. In the screenplay I said the Barber Shop looked haunted, and that's what I think every square inch of this world looks like – haunted. It's creepy. They are very unsettling sets to walk through because they're dark and they have strange, broken angles and you never quite know what might come round a corner, whether it's Sweeney Todd with a razor, Mrs Lovett with a pie, or Jack the Ripper. They're frightening sets, which is appropriate because it's a horror movie."

For the actors too, the sets were nothing short of inspiring. "I loved the sets," says Bonham Carter. "I always wanted to go back

to Victorian times although they're pretty dreadful in reality, but we can romanticize about them. I loved walking onto Fleet Street. The atmosphere, it does help you considerably if your environment invites your imagination to travel. And I loved my shop." In fact, Bonham Carter was consulted throughout the design and construction of Mrs Lovett's Pie Shop because her character has to move around it while making a pie and singing 'The Worst Pies in London'. "The props guys and the set people would ask, what kind of height for the counter? Where did I want to make the pie?" she explains. "Because in the space of very few lyrics I had to get rid of my knife, bring Sweeney in, sit him down and be back at the counter to start my pie on a certain beat. Sondheim wrote that song with all the propage in the beats so it had to be mapped out to the set."

While Burton has made several set-based films before, *Sweeney Todd* offered up a new set of challenges, simply because the vast majority of the story takes place in just two locations: Mrs Lovett's Pie Shop and Sweeney's Barber Shop, both very confined spaces. "It's a very interiorized movie," he notes. "Obviously we tried to open it up a bit so it doesn't feel like a stage show, but it was very limited. That's why it's a different kind of movie for me, to let things be on another kind of level and not so frenetic and little bit more interior, matching the characters, to let the events unfold. It felt like a different structure of a movie for me in that sense, and I let a lot of it play on

the actors and not worry so much about the flamboyance of the sets, just let them be a texture and a part of it, and open it up enough to breathe every now and again."

Having music playing on set, he says, certainly helped in that regard. "You'd put on the music and it would just suggest a camera move," he reveals. "It was important not to make it like an MTV kind of a thing, to keep the movements part of it but not overdo it. But the music certainly suggests movement

and camera moves. I can see why people use music on set, and I would consider it again, doing something to music, even if it's not a musical. It suggests a rhythm to a shot or a move or an angle that's quite fun to deal with, and makes you go quicker in a funny way."

Much as he had done with *Sleepy Hollow*, Burton wanted *Sweeney Todd* to be almost black and white, devoid of virtually all color. "The first idea was to make the film as close to black and white as possible," explains director of photography Dariusz Wolski. "Tim showed me a lot of old horror films. We both like film noir. We like old black and white movies. So that was the general approach, to make it very moody, very dark, a lot of contrast, very graphic. Dante builds sets that are very monochromatic, very stark. Then I come with lighting. We looked at a lot of photographs of old London. We tried to make the film look like an old movie with

Previous spread above:
Anthony stands across from Judge Turpin's mansion, on the London street set built by Dante Ferretti at Pinewood.

Previous spread opposite top:
The ballroom at Judge Turpin's house – one of the few sets to contain any color.

Previous spread opposite bottom:
A model of Turpin's study set.

Above:
More blood, please. Tim Burton knows exactly how much red stuff is required for the Beggar Woman's bleed out.

Opposite top:
A model of the ship Sweeney and Anthony arrive in.

Opposite bottom:
Sweeney's arrival, as seen on screen.

contemporary technology – a modern way of making an old-fashioned film."

That noir-like approach extended to sometimes shooting Sweeney Todd completely in silhouette. "When Johnny walks into the Pie Shop for the first time, Tim told me, I don't want to see him," Wolski reveals. It's dawn. You barely see outside. Mrs Lovett is cooking away. And Johnny walks in and you can hardly see him. Nevertheless, you can still feel his performance because he's just so good, having him in close-up, just seeing a little glint in his eye, and the way he turns his head completely works."

Later, in post-production, the Polish-born cinematographer would use the Digital Intermediate process to strip out even more color. "Saturation is color, so if you desaturate you take the color away," Wolski explains. "What we're doing in this film is a combination of make-up, wardrobe, set design and me treating the film, pulling the color out. We're trying to make this movie almost black and white, except for some faded colors, here and there. And blood."

Ah yes, the blood.

Since Sweeney's method of dispatching his victims is slitting their throats with a razor, the results are messy, to say the least, with at least eleven falling foul of Todd's instrument.

"The first time Tim and I met, the first thing we talked about was when we first saw *Sweeney Todd* on stage and how much we remember the blood," notes Logan. "At the first throat-slitting, the razor goes wide, the blood arched across the stage, the light hit it and it was this unique red."

"We made probably maybe sixty, seventy gallons of blood for our tests," says special effects supervisor Joss Williams, whose credits include *Munich* and *Charlie and the Chocolate Factory*. "And for filming purposes, we had a stock of probably twenty or thirty gallons for ourselves. We gave the props department some twenty gallons for dressing, and the prosthetics department, I think, probably twenty or thirty gallons. That's quite a lot."

"The effects in this film are very gory," says prosthetics supervisor Neal Scanlan, whose team were responsible for designing and executing the blood effects and throat cuttings. "However, what we're trying to do is push the boundaries to make it slightly ludicrous, and by doing that you take the audience away from that feeling that this is real. We're trying to push it to get to that Hammer horror feel and at the same time keep with the tone of the way Johnny and the actors are playing it."

Even so, copious blood and slit throats means an R-rating, almost unheard of for a musical.

"Tim made it a part of his deal when he signed on that it would be an R, because he didn't want to make the picture if it wasn't an R," says Richard Zanuck of the film's rating. "There was no way of doing this properly as a PG-13."

"First note we said to the studio was, 'Guys, don't even mention blood, there's going to be blood in the movie,'" Burton recalls, "because I had seen several stage productions since where they would tone down the blood and you go, 'Don't bother.' You can't be politically correct with this because it's a story about a serial killer and they cook people in pies. Don't try and soften it. But it's not overly graphic. It's all done in a Hammeresque way, it's not done in a *Hostel* way. The blood is bright red. It goes back to the show where it's more of a symbol and a part of the fabric of the color scheme."

"It is, in the classical dramatic sense, a blood tragedy," notes Logan. "Obviously it pays homage to Grand Guignol, it pays homage to the Penny Dreadfuls of Victorian London. But it's important to say that the blood in *Sweeney Todd* is not sadistic, it is not unnecessary, it is absolutely a part of the world that these characters inhabit, so to shy away from it would be dishonest and coy in a way this story is not and this filmmaker is not. The truth of this is, people are being killed, this central character is motivated with so much desire and passion that he has to kill people with his hands, and their blood gets on his hands and on his face, and he is coated with it – figuratively and literally."

EPILOGUE: A BEAUTIFUL MARRIAGE

In a London editing room in the summer of 2007, in the city in which he first saw Sondheim's musical so many years ago, Tim Burton is putting the finishing touches to the project he's been carrying around with him in one way or another since he was a student. And while Burton has never been a man for making proclamations or predictions about his work, it's readily apparent that he's in a very happy place regarding his version of *Sweeney Todd: The Demon Barber of Fleet Street*.

"There's always a possibility it might upset the purists because it's not the show, and there are numbers that are not in it," he admits. "I'm trying to be as pure to it as possible, but I don't know how the purists will respond to it. Then again, how many purists are there? A movie like this is a strange gamble because it's an R-rated musical, it's got blood in it, and people that go to Broadway shows don't usually go to see slasher films, and people who see slasher films don't usually go to Broadway shows."

"What's great about this movie," says Johnny Depp, "is that it's a beautiful marriage of two completely different worlds: the structure and the melody and that kind of operatic Broadway world, the Sondheim world. And then you have Tim and his kind of deconstruction and re-sculpting of it. He's really outdone himself, which I never thought possible, after some of his past work. But he's outdone himself. He's amazing."

"What I'm most excited about is that people who have never heard of Stephen Sondheim, who have never been to a Broadway show in their life, are going to get to see this majestic piece of work," says John Logan, who has cherished this material for as long as Burton, if not longer. "They're going to get to hear a score unlike anything that has ever been composed by an American composer. They're going to get to see a story that is unique, that they don't know. And they're going to get to understand why we, who love Sweeney Todd, have loved it for so long and so passionately. In a way they will get to be John Logan or Tim Burton watching this for the first time and being inspired with a passion that has lasted twenty-five years. At its heart *Sweeney Todd* is a horror musical. It is also a riveting character drama. It is also a wonderful black comedy. It is an exercise in Guignol. But, above everything, it is pure entertainment. It is the genius of Stephen Sondheim, the genius of Tim Burton, the world of Sweeney Todd coming together to create something unique and, I hope, very entertaining to a lot of people."

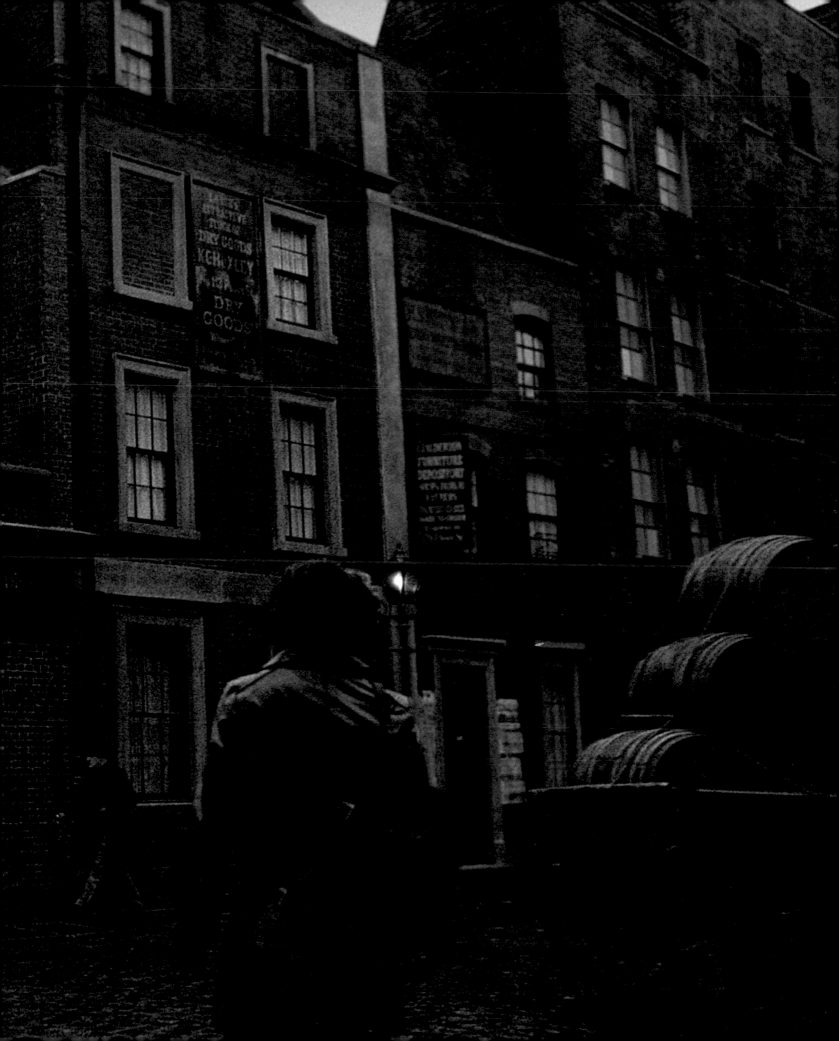

"Attend the Tale..."

The Illustrated Story

Top:
Concept art for London rooftops by Simon McGuire.

Right:
Concept art for London docks by Simon McGuire.

Opposite top:
Concept art for London scenes by Simon McGuire.

Opposite bottom:
Concept sketch of alleyway detail.

Far right:
Concept art for Fleet Street by Simon McGuire.

FINNISH AS BRICK COPPING

BELL LANE

TODD

*There's a hole in the world
Like a great black pit
And the vermin of the world
Inhabit it
And its morals aren't worth
What a pig could spit
And it goes by the name Of London.
At the top of the hole
Sit the privileged few
Making mock of the vermin
In the lower zoo,
Turning beauty into filth and greed.
I too
Have sailed the world, and seen its wonders
For the cruelty of men
Is as wondrous as Peru,
But there's no place like London!*

TODD

There was a barber and his wife,
And she was beautiful,
A foolish barber and his wife,
She was his reason and his life,
And she was beautiful,
And she was virtuous.
And he was...
Naïve.

TODD

There was another man who saw
That she was beautiful,
A pious vulture of the law,
Who with a gesture of his claw
Removed the barber from his plate.
Then there was nothing but to wait
And she would fall,
So soft,
So young,
So lost,
And oh, so beautiful!

Far left:
Sweeney Todd, his wife Lucy, and their baby Johanna in happier times.

Top:
The stern, saturnine figure of Judge Turpin casts his lascivious eye over Lucy.

Middle:
A sketch by Dante Ferretti of the flower market.

Bottom:
Judge Turpin makes his evil plans.

Top:

A concept design sketch by Dante Ferretti of the fancy dress ball that the Beadle brings Lucy to.

Left:

One of the sinister masked guests who buffet and confuse Lucy as she wanders through the swirling dancers at the ball.

Right:

Lucy drinks and, thinking the Judge has repented, asks: "Oh, where is Judge Turpin?"

Opposite:

The Beadle leads Lucy through the party to Judge Turpin.

MRS LOVETT
These are probably the worst pies in London.
I know why nobody cares to take them–
I should know,
I make them.
But good? No,
The worst pies in London–
Even that's polite.
The worst pies in London–
If you doubt it, take a bite.

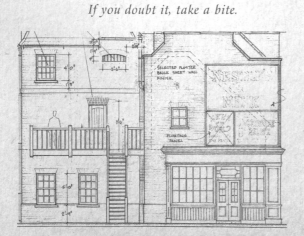

MRS. LOVETT

So it is you – Benjamin Barker.

TODD

Where's Lucy?! Where's my wife?!

MRS. LOVETT

She poisoned herself. Arsenic from the apothecary on the corner. I tried to stop her but she wouldn't listen to me. And he's got your daughter.

TODD

He? Judge Turpin?

MRS. LOVETT

Adopted her like his own.

TODD ABSORBS THIS SICKENING NEWS.

TODD

Fifteen years of sweating in a living hell on a false charge. Fifteen years dreaming that I might come home to find a loving wife and child...

A BEAT AS HE STARES INTO THE FIRE, MADNESS AND PURPOSE CREEPING IN.

MRS. LOVETT

Well, I can't say the years have been particularly kind to you, Mr. Barker, but you still–

TODD

No, not Barker. That man is dead. It's Todd now. Sweeney Todd ... And he will have his revenge.

HE CONTINUES WITH A CHILLING AND QUIET RESOLVE AS HE STARES WITH UNBLINKING EYES INTO THE FIRE:

TODD

Judge Turpin and the Beadle will pay for what they did.

A BEAT. HE FINALLY TURNS TO HER.

TODD

First I must have my shop back.

Opposite
top:
A downcast Mrs Lovett ponders where the meat for her pies is going to come from.

*Opposite
left:*
A blueprint of the Pie Shop facade.

*Opposite
right:*
A tormented Sweeney Todd listens to Mrs Lovett.

Bottom:
Mrs Lovett tells Sweeney the sorry story of what happened to his wife, Lucy, and their daughter Johanna.

TODD

These are my friends,
See how they glisten.
See this one shine,
How he smiles in the light.
My friend, my faithful friend.
Speak to me friend,
Whisper, I'll listen.
I know, I know –
You've been locked out of sight
All these years –
Like me, my friend.
Well, I've come home
To find you waiting.
Home,
And we're together,
And we'll do wonders,
Won't we?

JOHANNA

My cage has many rooms,
Damask and dark.
Nothing there sings,
Not even my lark.
Larks never will, you know,
When they're captive.
Teach me to be more adaptive.
Green finch and linnet bird,
Nightingale, blackbird,
Teach me how to sing.
If I cannot fly,
Let me sing.

BEGGAR WOMAN

'Ow would you like a little muff, dear,
A little jig jig
A little bounce around the bush?
Wouldn't you like to push me parsley?
It looks to me, dear,
Like you got plenty there to push.

Alms! ... Alms!...
For a desperate woman...

ANTHONY

I feel you,
Johanna,
I feel you.
I was half convinced I'd waken,
Satisfied enough to dream you.
Happily I was mistaken, Johanna!
I'll steal you,
Johanna,
I'll steal you...

Opposite
top:
Trapped like a bird in a cage, Johanna is a prisoner in Judge Turpin's Mayfair mansion.

Opposite
bottom:
Concept sketch by Dante Ferretti of the interior of Johanna's room.

Top:
While out walking, Anthony is accosted by a Beggar Woman.

Bottom:
It's love at first sight when Anthony sees Johanna. "They are, in many ways, the only innocent characters in the entire world of Sweeney Todd," says writer/producer John Logan of Anthony and Johanna.

JUDGE

A sailor, eh?

ANTHONY

Yes, sir. The "Bountiful" out of Plymouth.

JUDGE
(HANDING HIM A SNIFTER OF BRANDY)

A sailor must know the ways of the world, yes?
... Must be practiced in the ways of the world
... Would you say you are practiced, boy?

ANTHONY

Sir?

THE JUDGE MOVES TO CONSIDER SOME BEAUTIFUL
VOLUMES, BOUND IN THE RICHEST LEATHER. HE RUNS
A FINGER ALONG THE SPINES OF THE BOOKS; HIS LARGE
LIBRARY OF PORNOGRAPHY.

JUDGE

Oh, yes ... such practices ... the geishas of Japan
... the concubines of Siam .. the catamites of
Greece ... the harlots of India ... I have them
all here ... Drawings of them....

(HE TURNS AGAIN TO ANTHONY)

... All the vile things you've done with your
whores.

ANTHONY IS SPEECHLESS. THE JUDGE JUST SMILES AT HIM
AMIABLY.

JUDGE

Would you like to see?

Top:
Anthony comes to see
Judge Turpin in his
book-lined study...

Bottom:
Is offered a look
at his collection of
pornography...

*Opposite
top:*
Is viciously threatened
by the Judge....

*Opposite
bottom:*
Then tossed out on the
street by the Beadle
and told never to
return. .

ANTHONY
(STANDING)
I think there's been some mistake –

JUDGE
Oh, I think not. You gandered at my ward, Johanna … You gandered at her … Yes, sir, you gandered.

THE BEADLE MOVES BEHIND ANTHONY.

ANTHONY
(GLANCING NERVOUSLY BACK AT THE BEADLE)
I meant no harm –

JUDGE
Your meaning is immaterial. Mark me: if I see your face again on this street, you'll rue the day your bitch of a mother gave you birth.

ANTHONY IS STUNNED. THE JUDGE PROCEEDS WITH SHOCKING VENOM:

JUDGE
My Johanna isn't one of your bloody cock-chafers! My Johanna is not to be gandered at!

TOBY

Buy Pirelli's Miracle Elixir:
Anything wot's slick, sir,
Soon sprouts curls.
Try Pirelli's!
When they see how thick, sir,
You can have your pick, sir,
Of the girls!

MRS. LOVETT
(SNIFFING ANOTHER CUSTOMER'S BOTTLE)

What is this?

TODD

Smells like piss.

Top:
Pirelli's young assistant
Toby extols the virtues
of his master's miracle
elixir.

Bottom:
An early concept sketch
for Pirelli's portable
barber's shop by Simon
McGuire.

Opposite:
Sweeney sniffs out the
secret ingredient in
Pirelli's elixir – piss!

PIRELLI

I am Adolfo Pirelli,
Da king of da barbers, da barber of kings,
E buon giorno, good day,
I blow you a kiss!
And I, da so-famous Pirelli,
I wish-a to know-a
Who has-a da nerve-a to say
My elixir is piss!
Who says this?!

TODD
You see these razors?

MRS. LOVETT
(TO THE CROWD)
The finest in England.

TODD
(GLARING AT PIRELLI)
I lay them against five pounds you are no match for me. You hear me, sir? Either accept my challenge or reveal yourself as a sham.

PIRELLI

To shave-a da face,
To trim-a da beard,
To make-a da bristle
Clean like a whistle,
Dis is from early infancy
Da talent give to me
By God!
         (CROSSES HIMSELF WITH HIS RAZOR)
It take-a da skill,
It take-a da brains,
It take-a da will
To take-a da pains,
It take-a da pace,
It take-a da graaaaaace...

WHILE PIRELLI HOLDS THIS NOTE ELABORATELY, TODD,
WITH A FEW DEFT STROKES, QUICKLY LATHERS HIS
MAN'S FACE, SHAVES HIM AND SIGNALS THE BEADLE TO
EXAMINE HIM.

BEADLE
(BLOWING WHISTLE)
The winner is Todd.

PIRELLI DEFLATES.

MRS. LOVETT
(FEELING THE CUSTOMER'S CHEEK)
Smooth as a baby's arse! – (TO TODD) – Well done, dear!

THE CROWD LAUGHS AND APPLAUDS TODD AS PIRELLI GOES TO HIM:

PIRELLI
(A PROFOUND BOW)
Sir, I bow to a skill far defter than my own.

TODD
The five pounds.

PIRELLI PRODUCES A DISTINCTIVE CHATELAINE PURSE AND REMOVES A FIVE POUND NOTE, GIVES IT TO TODD:

PIRELLI
Here, sir. And may the good Lord smile on you –
(A QUICK STAB OF A SMILE)
– Until we meet again.

TODD
And the Judge? When will we get to him?

MRS. LOVETT
Can't you think of nothing else? Always broodin' away on yer wrongs what happened heaven knows how many years ago...

Slow, love, slow
Time's so fast
Now, goes quickly
See, now it's past!
Soon will come,
Soon will last.
Wait.
Don't you know,
Silly man,
Half the fun is to
Plan the plan?
All good things come to
Those who can
Wait.

PIRELLI

Mr. Todd.

TODD

Signor Pirelli.

PIRELLI
(REVERTING TO HIS NATURAL IRISH)

Call me Danny. Daniel Higgins' the name when it's not professional... I'd like me five quid back, if'n ya don't mind.

TODD

Why?

PIRELLI

Because you entered into our little wager on false pretenses, me friend ... And so you might remember to be more forthright in the future, you'll be handing over half your profits to me, share and share alike...

TODD SHAKES HIS HEAD, AMUSED, AND BEGINS TO TURN AWAY WHEN PIRELLI SAYS:

PIRELLI

... Mr. Benjamin Barker.

Left and opposite: Early sketches of Judge Turpin and Sweeney Todd.

Right: Judge Turpin, in need of a shave, arrives at Sweeney's shop.

Opposite: Sweeney with another of his friends; "I always thought of Sweeney's razor like King Arthur's Excalibur," says Logan.

TODD

And what may I do for you today, sir? A stylish trimming of the hair? A soothing skin massage?

JUDGE

You see, sir, a man infatuate with love,
Her ardent and eager slave.
So fetch the pomade and pumice stone
And lend me a more seductive tone,
A sprinkling perhaps of French cologne,
But first, sir, I think – a shave.

TODD

The closest I ever gave.

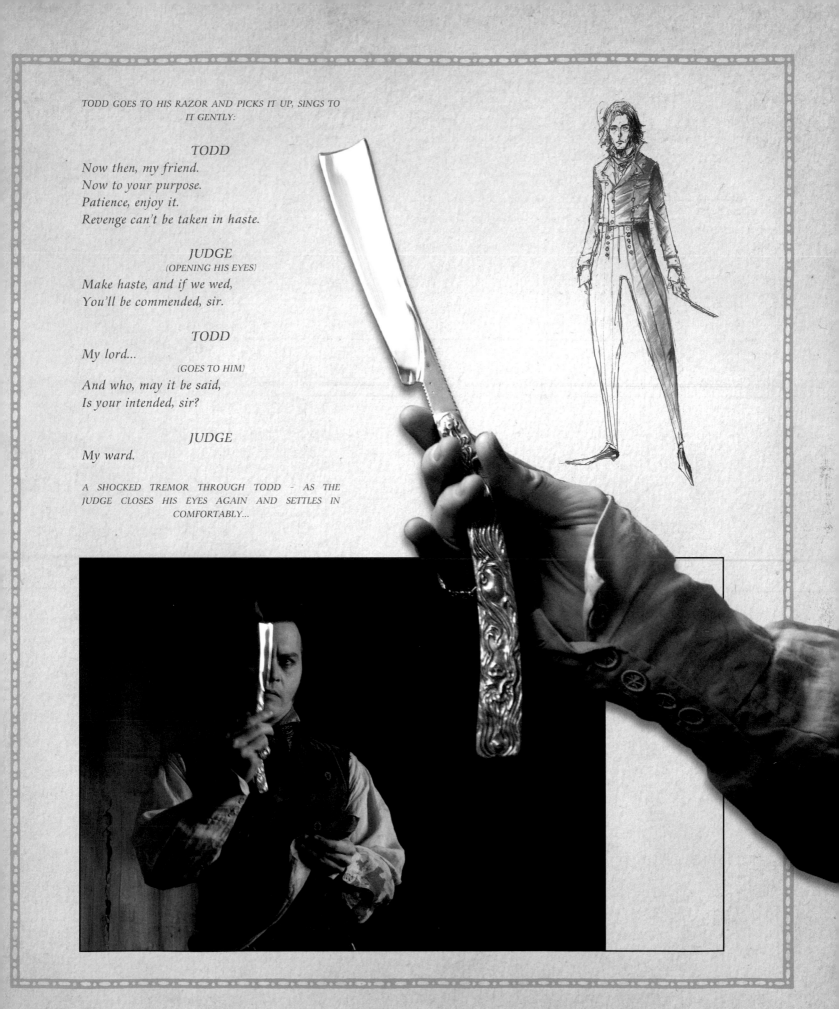

TODD GOES TO HIS RAZOR AND PICKS IT UP, SINGS TO
IT GENTLY:

TODD
Now then, my friend.
Now to your purpose.
Patience, enjoy it.
Revenge can't be taken in haste.

JUDGE
(OPENING HIS EYES)
Make haste, and if we wed,
You'll be commended, sir.

TODD
My lord...
(GOES TO HIM)
And who, may it be said,
Is your intended, sir?

JUDGE
My ward.

A SHOCKED TREMOR THROUGH TODD – AS THE
JUDGE CLOSES HIS EYES AGAIN AND SETTLES IN
COMFORTABLY...

THE MUSIC APPROACHES A FEVERISH CRESCENDO AS
TODD PREPARES TO FINALLY KILL THE JUDGE AND THEY
SING SIMULTANEOUSLY:

JUDGE

Pretty women, yes!
Pretty women, sir!
Pretty women!
Pretty women, sir!

TODD

Pretty women, here's to
Pretty women, all the
Pretty women –

JUST AS THE MUSIC REACHES A CLIMAX, TODD RAISES
HIS ARM IN A HUGE ARC AND IS ABOUT TO SLASH THE
JUDGE'S THROAT WHEN –

SUDDENLY –

ANTHONY BURSTS IN –

Top:
Murder interruptus. Just
as Todd's about to make
his mark on Turpin's
neck...

Bottom:
Anthony bursts in.

Opposite:
On hearing of Anthony's
plan to elope with
Johanna, Turpin storms
out. But not before
promising to lock up his
ward in a place Anthony
will never find her.

ANTHONY

Mr. Todd! I've seen Johanna! She said she'll leave with me tonight –!

THE JUDGE JUMPS UP, AWAY FROM TODD –

JUDGE

You! – There is indeed a higher power to warn me thus in time –

HE TEARS OFF THE SHEET AS HE ADVANCES SAVAGELY ON ANTHONY:

JUDGE

Johanna elope with you? Deceiving slut! – I'll lock her up in some obscure retreat where neither you nor any other vile creature shall ever lay eyes on her again!

HE SPINS WITH VENOM TO TODD:

JUDGE

And as for you, barber, it is all too clear what company you keep. Service them well and hold their custom – for you'll have none of mine.

HE STRIDES OUT.

TODD

And I will get him back
Even as he gloats.
In the meantime I'll practice
On less honorable throats –

TODD SUDDENLY FALLS TO HIS KNEES, KEENING IN
ANGUISH –

TODD

And my Lucy lies in ashes
And I'll never see my girl again,
But the work waits, I'm alive at last
(A FINAL EXALTED CRY)

And I'm full of *JOOOOOOY!!*

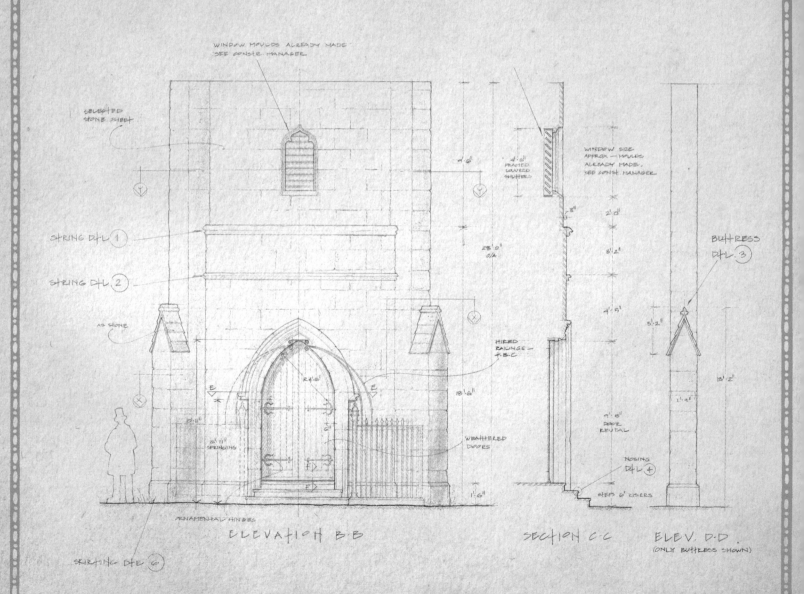

Previous spread:
Todd wails in agony after failing to kill Judge Turpin.

Top:
Mrs Lovett hatches a plan to put Sweeney's unwanted corpses to good use.

Bottom:
The exterior and interior of Mrs Lovett's Pie Shop, built on Pinewood's S Stage.

Opposite:
Todd delights at Mrs Lovett's gruesome idea.

MRS. LOVETT

Seems an awful waste...
Such a nice plump frame
Wot's-his-name
Has...
Had...
Has...
Nor it can't be traced.
Business needs a lift –
Debts to be erased –
Think of it as thrift,

As a gift...
If you get my drift...
(TODD HAS NO IDEA WHAT SHE IS TALKING ABOUT)
No?
(SHE SIGHS)
Seems an awful waste.
I mean,
With the price of meat what it is,
When you get it,
If you get it –

TODD SUDDENLY UNDERSTANDS:

TODD

Ah!

MRS. LOVETT

Good, you got it.
(SHE WARMS TO THE IDEA)
Take, for instance,
Mrs. Mooney and her pie shop.
Business never better, using only
Pussycats and toast.
And a pussy's good for maybe six or
Seven at the most.
And I'm sure they can't compare
As far as taste –

TODD

Mrs. Lovett,
What a charming notion,

THE MUSIC BUILDS AS THEY SING SIMULTANEOUSLY:

TODD

Eminently practical and yet
Appropriate as always.
Mrs. Lovett, how I've lived without you
All these years I'll never know!
How delectable!
Also undetectable.
How choice!
How rare!

MRS. LOVETT

Well, it does seem a
Waste...
It's an idea...
Think about it...
Lots of other gentlemen'll
Soon be coming for a shave,
Won't they?
Think of
All them
Pies!

TODD

What is that?

MRS. LOVETT

It's fop.
Finest in the shop.
Or we have some shepherd's pie peppered
With actual shepherd
On top.
And I've just begun.
Here's a politician – so oily
It's served with a doily –
Have one?

TODD

Put it on a bun.
(SHE LOOKS AT HIM QUIZZICALLY)
Well, you never know if it's going to run.

MRS. LOVETT

Try the friar.
Fried, it's drier.

TODD

No, the clergy is really
Too coarse and too mealy.

MRS. LOVETT

Then actor –
That's compacter.

TODD

Yes, and always arrives overdone.
(HE IS SUDDENLY DARK AND PURPOSEFUL)
I'll come again when you
Have Judge on the menu...

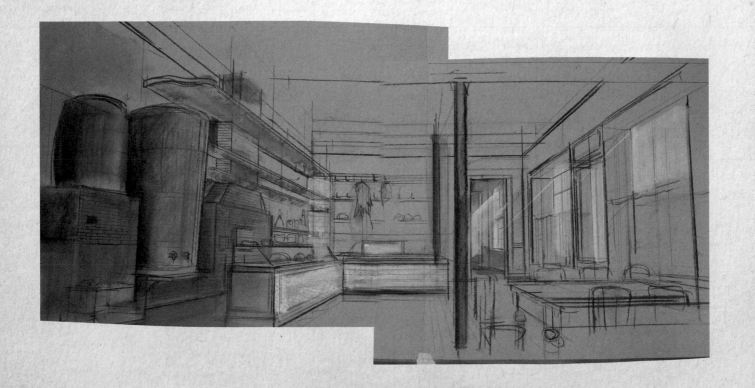

'SWEENEY TODD'

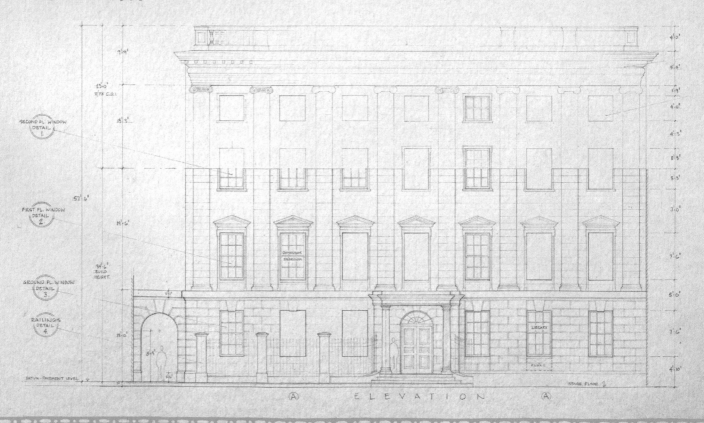

JOHANNA

Sir ... A gentlemen knocks before entering a lady's room.

JUDGE

Indeed he does ... But I see no lady.

HE ENTERS, DANGEROUSLY QUIET. AND TERRIFICALLY HURT.

JUDGE

I told myself the sailor was lying ... I told myself this was a cruel fiction ... That my Johanna would never betray me. Never hurt me so.

HE MOVES TOWARD HER. SHE STANDS HER GROUND.

JOHANNA

Sir ... I will leave this place.

JUDGE

I think that only appropriate. Since you no longer find my company to your liking, madam, we shall provide you with new lodgings.

HE STANDS VERY CLOSE TO HER. STILL SHE HOLDS HER GROUND.

JUDGE

Until this moment I have spared the rod ... And the ungrateful child has broken my heart. Now you will learn discipline...

THE LARGE FORM OF THE BEADLE FILLS THE DOORWAY. SHE GLANCES TO HIM, DISQUIETED.

JUDGE

When you have learned to appreciate what you have, perhaps we shall meet again. Until then ... Think on your sins.

Opposite top:
Judge Turpin catches Johanna in the act of packing to elope with Anthony.

Opposite bottom:
Architectural plans for the Judge's Mayfair mansion.

Right:
The original sketches for the costumes worn by Alan Rickman and Jayne Wisener in this scene.

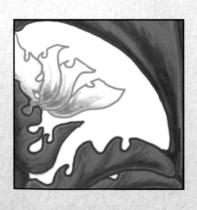

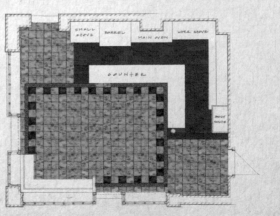

Top:
Concept sketch for the exterior eating area of the Pie Shop.

Bottom:
A tile from the Pie Shop interior and plans for the floor layout in the Pie Shop.

Opposite:
Mrs Lovett looks on as Toby ejects the Beggar Woman from the Pie Shop..

TOBY

Ladies and gentlemen,
You can't imagine the rapture in store –
         (INDICATING THE PIE SHOP)
Just inside of this door!
There you'll sample
Mrs. Lovett's meat pies,
Savory and sweet pies,
As you'll see.
You who eat pies,
Mrs. Lovett's meat pies
Conjure up the treat pies
Used to be!

MRS. LOVETT

Nice to see you, dearie...
How have you been keeping?...
Cor, me bones is weary!
Toby –!

      (INDICATING A CUSTOMER)
One for the gentleman...
Hear the birdies cheeping –
Helps to keep it cheery...

SHE SPOTS THE BEGGAR WOMAN APPROACHING AND
    RESPONDS WITH UNUSUAL FEROCITY:

MRS. LOVETT

Toby!
Throw the old woman out!

CUSTOMERS

God, that's good!

MRS. LOVETT

What's my secret?
> (TO A WOMAN)

Frankly, dear – forgive my candor–
Family secret,
All to do with herbs.
Things like being
Careful with your coriander,
That's what makes the gravy grander –!

THE CUSTOMERS ARE GETTING MORE RABID NOW
– STUFFING IN THE GORGEOUS MEAT PIES IN GREAT
FISTFULS –

CUSTOMERS

More hot pies!
More hot!
More pies!

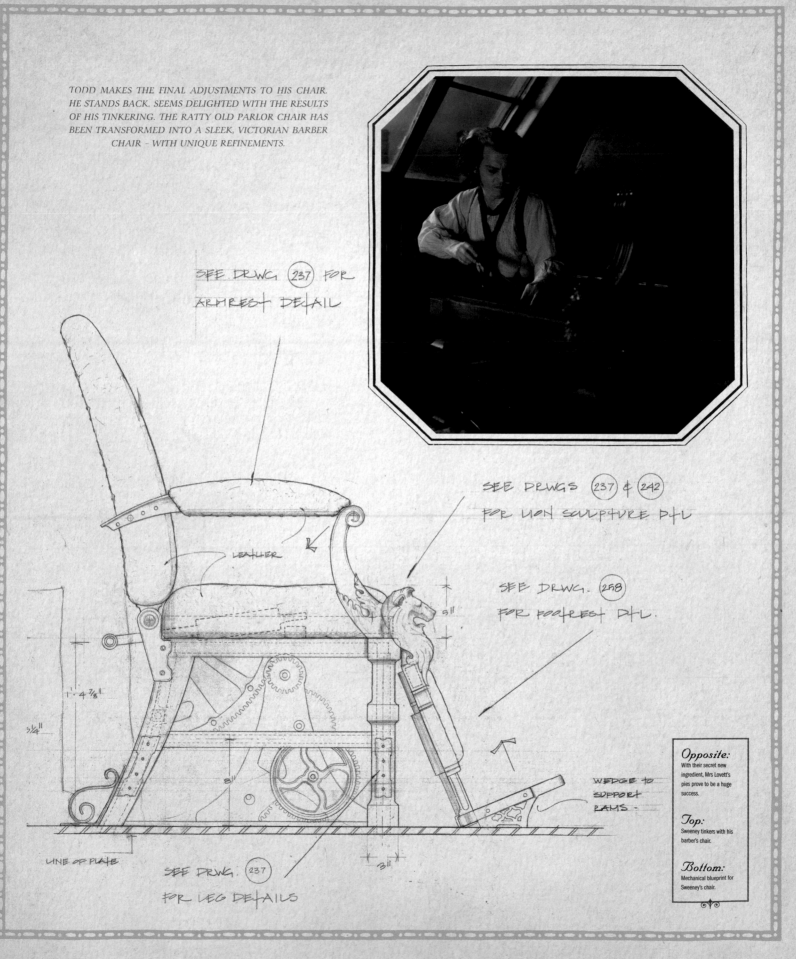

TODD MAKES THE FINAL ADJUSTMENTS TO HIS CHAIR.
HE STANDS BACK. SEEMS DELIGHTED WITH THE RESULTS
OF HIS TINKERING. THE RATTY OLD PARLOR CHAIR HAS
BEEN TRANSFORMED INTO A SLEEK, VICTORIAN BARBER
CHAIR - WITH UNIQUE REFINEMENTS.

SEE DRWG (237) FOR
ARMREST DETAIL

SEE DRWGS (237) & (242)
FOR LION SCULPTURE DTL

SEE DRWG. (258)
FOR FOOTREST DTL.

LEATHER

WEDGE TO
SUPPORT
RAMS

LINE OF PLATE

SEE DRWG. (237)
FOR LEG DETAILS

Opposite:
With their secret new
ingredient, Mrs Lovett's
pies prove to be a huge
success.

Top:
Sweeney tinkers with his
barber's chair.

Bottom:
Mechanical blueprint for
Sweeney's chair.

Left:
Anthony scours London for Johanna.

Opposite:
Concept art for the docks by Simon McGuire.

Bottom:
Concept art for the Old Bailey at night by Simon McGuire.

WE DISCOVER ANTHONY, SEARCHING THROUGH THE STREETS FOR JOHANNA.

ANTHONY
I feel you, Johanna,
I feel you.
Do they think that walls can hide you?
Even now I'm at your window.
I am in the dark beside you,
Buried sweetly in your yellow hair,
Johanna...

HE CONTINUES WALKING...

EXT. ASYLUM - NIGHT

...ANTHONY WANDERS PAST THE HIGH AND IMPENETRABLE WALLS OF A MADHOUSE, THE DEMENTED SOULS WITHIN CAN BE SEEN MOVING ABOUT IN SILHOUETTE BEHIND BARRED WINDOWS.

ANTHONY

I feel you...
Johanna...

SOMETHING MAKES HIM STOP. HE TURNS TO CONSIDER THE ASYLUM...

Opposite top:
Anthony walks past the hanging carcasses of the busy meat market.

Opposite bottom:
Concept sketch for the opium den by Simon McGuire.

Top:
Opium den image by Simon McGuire.

Bottom:
Anthony moves down a dark alley. Shadowy figures lurk along the alley walls.

...TODD SHAVES ANOTHER CUSTOMER. A BEAUTIFUL
MORNING OUTSIDE THE WINDOW.

TODD
Wake up, Johanna!
Another bright red day!
(HE SLITS THE CUSTOMER'S THROAT)
We learn, Johanna,
To say...
Goodbye...

AS THE NOTE CONTINUES, HE PULLS THE LEVER AND THE
CUSTOMER DISAPPEARS DOWN THE CHUTE...

MRS. LOVETT

I've always had this dream of living at the seaside ... I got a picture postcard from me Aunt Nettie once. Oh, it seems like such a grand place...

(NOTES TOBY FLYING HIS KITE)

And all that fresh aquatic air's bound to be good for the lad's poxy lungs...
By the sea, Mr. Todd,
That's the life I covet;
By the sea, Mr. Todd,
Ooh, I know you'd love it!
You and me, Mr. T.,
We could be alone
In a house wot we'd almost own
Down by the sea...

TODD

(GRUMBLES)

Anything you say.

MRS. LOVETT

Wouldn't that be smashing?

MRS. LOVETT AND TODD GETTING MARRIED. THIS BEING HER FANTASY, AFTER ALL, SHE WEARS WHITE. TODD IS IN A CONSTRICTING MORNING COAT WITH A RAKISH TOP HAT. TOBY, THE BEST MAN, WATCHES PROUDLY.

MRS. LOVETT (V.O.)
But a seaside wedding
Could be devised,
Me rumpled bedding
Legitimized.

THEY EXCHANGE VOWS AND KISS.

MRS. LOVETT (V.O.)
My eyelids'll flutter,
I'll turn into butter,
The moment I mutter
"I do-hoo!"

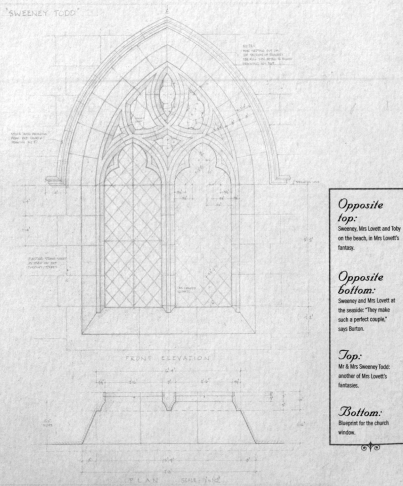

Opposite top:
Sweeney, Mrs Lovett and Toby on the beach, in Mrs Lovett's fantasy.

Opposite bottom:
Sweeney and Mrs Lovett at the seaside: "They make such a perfect couple," says Burton.

Top:
Mr & Mrs Sweeney Todd: another of Mrs Lovett's fantasies.

Bottom:
Blueprint for the church window.

TODD
You've found Johanna?

ANTHONY
For all the good it'll do – it's impossible to get to her.

TODD BEGINS PACING, THE TIGER AGAIN, HIS MIND IS RACING –

TODD
A madhouse ... A madhouse ... Where?

ANTHONY
Fogg's Asylum. But I've circled the place a dozen times. There's no way in. It's a fortress.

ANTHONY FADES TO A BROODING SILENCE AS TODD CONTINUES PACING, THINKING, THINKING. MRS. LOVETT WATCHES HIM, CONCERNED.

TODD SUDDENLY STOPS...

WE SEE HIM SETTLING INTO AN INSPIRED SORT OF CALM, AS IF HE CAN FINALLY SEE THE PROMISED LAND.

TODD
(A WHISPER)

I've got him.

ANTHONY

Mr. Todd?

TODD
(TO ANTHONY)

We've got her ... Where do you suppose all the wigmakers of London go to obtain their human hair? Bedlam. They get their hair from the lunatics at Bedlam –

ANTHONY

I don't understand –

TODD SUDDENLY GRABS ANTHONY AND HAULS HIM UP – HOLDS HIM CLOSE, FOREHEAD TO FOREHEAD – HIS WHISPERED INTENSITY TRULY DISTURBING:

TODD

We shall set you up as a wigmaker's apprentice in search of hair – that will gain you access – then you will take her.

ANTHONY

Yes...

TODD

You will not be deterred – You will slaughter the world – To bring her here.

Opposite:
Anthony reveals that he's found Johanna locked away inside a madhouse.

Bottom:
Concept sketch of Fogg's Asylum by Dante Ferretti.

TOBY

That's Signor Pirelli's purse!

MRS. LOVETT

No, no, love – this is just something Mr. T. give me for my birthday –

TOBY

See that proves it – what I been thinkin'–
(HE STANDS, URGENTLY PULLING HER HAND)
We gotta go, ma'am, right now – we gotta find the Beadle and get the law here –

SHE PULLS HIM DOWN TO HER AGAIN, AGITATED, HER MIND RACING:

MRS. LOVETT

Hush now, Toby, hush ... Here, you just sit next to me nice and quiet ...
(CALMING)
... How could you think such a thing of Mr. Todd, who's been so good to us?

HE CALMS DOWN A BIT AS SHE HOLDS HIM.

MRS. LOVETT

Nothing's gonna harm you,
Not while I'm around.
Nothing's gonna harm you, darling,
Not while I'm around.

TOBY

Demons'll charm you
With a smile
For a while,
But in time
Nothing's gonna harm you,
Not while I'm around.

THE MUSIC CONTINUES AS SHE HOLDS HIM, AND SHE COMES TO A PAINFUL, DREADFUL DECISION. THERE ARE TEARS IN HER EYES.

MRS. LOVETT
(SOFTLY)

Funny we should be having this little chat

right now ... 'Cause I was just thinkin', you know how you've always fancied coming into the bakehouse with me to help make the pies?

TOBY
(DREAMILY)

Yes, ma'am.

SHE QUICKLY DRIES HER EYES AND THEN TURNS HIM TO LOOK AT HER.

MRS. LOVETT
(SMILES)

Well ... no time like the present.

THE BAKEHOUSE

A MACABRE VISION OF HELL.

THE ROOF HANGS LOW IN THIS SUBTERRANEAN CHAMBER. THE GRISLY TOOLS OF HER TRADE ARE SCATTERED ABOUT THE PLACE: A LARGE, STAINED CHOPPING BLOCK; A MEAT GRINDER; BUCKETS OF QUESTIONABLE VISCOUS LIQUID; CLEAVERS AND BONE SAWS AND MEAT HOOKS; WET SEWER GRATES FOR THE BLOOD.

A METAL SHEET, HINGED AT THE TOP, HAS BEEN ATTACHED TO COVER AN OPENING IN THE WALL: THE MOUTH OF THE CHUTE FROM THE BARBER SHOP ABOVE.

AND EERIEST OF ALL ... THE THUNDERING ROAR OF FLAME COMING FROM A LARGE INDUSTRIAL OVEN AGAINST ONE WALL.

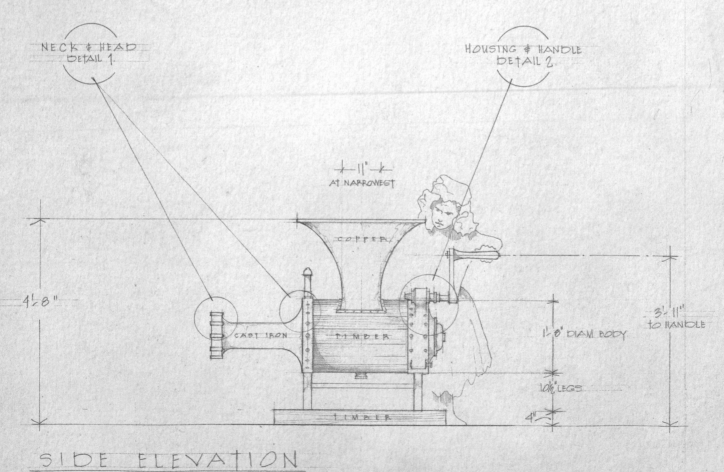

NECK & HEAD
DETAIL 1

HOUSING & HANDLE
DETAIL 2

11"
AT NARROWEST

COPPER

CAST IRON   TIMBER

4'-8"

3'-11"
TO HANDLE

1'-8" DIAM BODY

10½" LEGS

TIMBER

4"

SIDE ELEVATION

FOGG
I keep the blondes over here. It was yellow hair you was looking for, sir?

ANTHONY
Yes.

FOGG GOES INTO THE CROWDED CELL – THE INMATES, ALL BLONDE WOMEN, SCURRY BACK, CLEARLY TERRIFIED OF FOGG. ANTHONY SEES JOHANNA, WEARING A FILTHY STRAITJACKET, HUNCHED LIKE A FERAL ANIMAL, COWERING IN A CORNER OF THE CELL.

ANTHONY
(POINTS)
That one has hair the shade I need.

FOGG GOES TO FETCH JOHANNA, HAULS HER TO ANTHONY:

FOGG
Come, child. Smile for the gentleman and you shall have a sweetie.

Top:
Concept art for the exterior of Fogg's Asylum by Simon McGuire.

Bottom:
Posing as a wigmaker's assistant, Anthony follows Fogg through the bowels of the asylum, seeking out Johanna among the inmates.

Opposite top:
Fogg points out the blonde inmates to Anthony.

Opposite bottom:
Anthony takes his chance: he pulls a revolver from his clothing, grabs Johanna and they escape.

JOHANNA'S EYES SHOOT WIDE WHEN SHE SEES ANTHONY,
BUT SHE SAYS NOTHING.

FOGG
(PREPARES SCISSORS)
Now, where shall I cut?

BEFORE FOGG CAN REACT – ANTHONY PULLS A REVOLVER
FROM HIS CLOTHING, GRABS JOHANNA AND PUSHES
FOGG BACK INTO THE CELL.

HE SWINGS THE CELL DOOR SHUT, LOCKING FOGG IN.

ANTHONY
*Not a word, Mr. Fogg, or it will be your last
... Now, I leave you to the mercy of your
"children."*

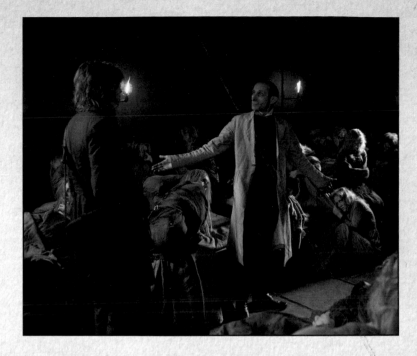

ANTHONY AND JOHANNA HURRY INTO THE BARBER SHOP. SHE IS NOW DRESSED AS A SCRUFFY BOY, A CAP HIDING HER HAIR. SHE IS DISTRACTED AND DISTURBED.

ANTHONY

Mr. Todd...? No matter. You wait for him here – I'll return with the coach in less than half an hour...

SHE GENTLY TOUCHES TODD'S COLLECTION OF RAZORS...

ANTHONY

Don't worry, darling, in those clothes, no one will recognize you ... You're safe now.

SHE PICKS UP THE LARGEST RAZOR, LOOKS AT IT, AN EERIE ECHO OF HER FATHER.

JOHANNA
(DARKLY IRONIC)

Safe ... So we run away and then all our dreams come true?

ANTHONY

I hope so...

JOHANNA

I have never had dreams. Only nightmares.

ANTHONY

Johanna ... When we're free of this place all the ghosts will go away.

She looks at him very intensely:

JOHANNA

No, Anthony, they never go away.

He gently touches her face.

ANTHONY

I'll be right back to you ... Half an hour and we'll be free.

HE GOES.

SHE TURNS TO THE WINDOW, WATCHES HIM GO. HER EXPRESSION IS SAD: HE WILL NEVER FULLY COMPREHEND HER DEPTH.

THEN SHE SEES THE BEGGAR WOMAN APPROACHING FROM ACROSS THE STREET...

Opposite:
Anthony and Johanna, disguised as a young boy, take refuge in Sweeney's shop.

Bottom:
From across the street, the Beggar Woman approaches.

TODD
Out of here! Now!

BEGGAR WOMAN
(REALLY PEERING AT HIM NOW)
Hey, don't I know you, mister?

TODD SUDDENLY SEES – THE JUDGE! – WALKING TOWARD
THE SHOP – TODD HAS NO TIME –!

THE MUSIC THUNDERS AS –

IN ONE BRUTAL MOTION – HE SWINGS AROUND AND
GRABS HIS RAZOR – FIERCELY SLASHES HER THROAT
– TOSSES HER IN THE CHAIR – PULLS THE LEVER – SHE
SLIDES THROUGH THE FLOOR – HE PULLS THE CHAIR
BACK TO ITS NORMAL POSITION JUST AS –

THE JUDGE ENTERS.

Top:
The Beggar Woman
confronts Sweeney...

Bottom:
But Sweeney has no time
for her. He slices her
throat, then sends her
down the secret chute
into the bakehouse, just
as Judge Turpin arrives,
looking for Johanna..

TODD

The years no doubt have changed me, sir. But then, I suppose the face of a barber – the face of a prisoner in the dock – is not particularly memorable.

JUDGE
(A HORRIFIED REALIZATION)

Benjamin Barker!

TODD

BENJAMIN BARKER!

Bottom:
Settling down for another shave, Turpin suddenly recognises Sweeney from across the years. Razor in hand, Sweeney finally takes his vengeance on the man who destroyed his life.

Next spread:
"It is a story about a man who seeks revenge. And in the process of achieving that revenge, goes mad," says Logan.

HIS QUEST IS COMPLETED.

HIS DEMONS SILENCED.

THE GHOSTS ARE GONE.

IT'S DONE.

HE JUST KNEELS THERE. NO REASON TO MOVE. NO PURPOSE IN LIFE.

THEN...

A SOUND FROM THE CHEST. A SLIGHT THUMP.

HIS EYES DART TO THE CHEST.

HE SLOWLY PICKS UP HIS RAZOR AND MOVES TO THE CHEST. THEN SUDDENLY WRENCHES IT OPEN AND HAULS OUT JOHANNA –

TODD
(DARKLY)
Come for a shave, have you, lad?

JOHANNA
No – I...

HE TOSSES HER IN THE CHAIR, THROWS BACK HIS ARM, HIS RAZOR READY –

TODD
Surely, yes! Everyone needs a good shave –!

SUDDENLY - A PIERCING SCREAM ECHOES UP FROM THE
CHUTE-

MRS. LOVETT'S VOICE - SCREAMING TO RAISE THE DEAD

TODD RIVETS JOHANNA, POINTING THE RAZOR AT HER,
A LETHAL WARNING:

TODD
Forget my face.

HE SPINS AND BOLTS OUT OF THE SHOP, LEAVING HER
SITTING IN THE CHAIR-

TODD
(LOOKING UP)
You lied to me...

MRS. LOVETT
(DESPERATELY)
No, no, not lied at all.
No, I never lied.

TODD
(TO BEGGAR WOMAN)
Lucy...

MRS. LOVETT
Said she took the poison – she did –
Never said that she died –
Poor thing,
She lived–

TODD
I've come home again...

MRS. LOVETT
But it left her weak in the head,
All she did for months was just lie there in bed–

TODD
Lucy...

MRS. LOVETT
Should've been in hospital,
Wound up in Bedlam instead,
Poor thing!

TODD
Oh, my God...

MRS. LOVETT
Better you should think she was dead.
(PASSIONATELY)
Yes, I lied 'cos I love you!

Top:
Toby has seen every-
thing. He slowly moves
and carefully picks up
Todd's razor...

Opposite:
As Benjamin Barker, the
naïve, foolish barber,
cradles the body of his
dead wife.

TODD
There was a barber and his wife,
And she was beautiful.
A foolish barber and his wife,
She was his reason and his life.
And she was beautiful.
And she was virtuous.
And he was...
Naive.

*A*ttend the tale of
Sweeney Todd!
He served a dark
and a hungry god!
To seek revenge
may lead to hell.
But everyone does it,
if seldom as well
As Sweeney...
As Sweeney Todd...
The Demon Barber of Fleet...
... Street!

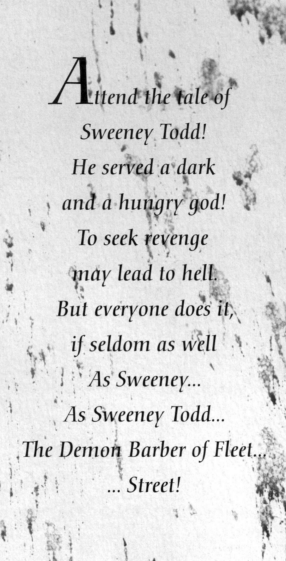

SWEENEY TODD
THE DEMON BARBER OF FLEET STREET
ISBN 1 84576 704 7
ISBN-13 9781845767044

Published by
Titan Books
A division of
Titan Publishing Group Ltd
144 Southwark St
London
SE1 0UP

First edition December 2007
2 4 6 8 10 9 7 5 3 1

Designed by Holly C. Kempf.
Photographs by Peter Mountain and Leah Gallo.

&ᔕ ACKNOWLEDGMENTS ᔕ

Titan Books would like to thank Mark Salisbury and Holly Kempf for taking on a tight deadline, and Risa Kessler, Chris Horton, Christina Hahni, Maren Moebius, Paul Ruditis and Abbie Wisdom at Paramount for their help on this project. Our gratitude also goes to the entire cast and crew of *Sweeney Todd*, especially to Derek Frey for his invaluable support, and of course Tim Burton for his enthusiasm, time and Foreword.

The author would like to thank Tim Burton, Richard Zanuck, Helena Bonham Carter, Johnny Depp, Patrick McCormick, Sarah Clark and Derek Frey for welcoming me into Sweeney's world. Special thanks also to Laura, Milo, Judith and my mum for their love and support, as well as a big thank you to the editorial team at Titan, especially Adam Newell, Cath Trechman and Katy Wild.

Visit our website:
www.titanbooks.com

Did you enjoy this book? We love to hear from our readers. Please e-mail us at: **readerfeedback@titanemail.com** or write to Reader Feedback at the above address.

To receive advance information, news, competitions, and exclusive Titan offers online, please register as a member by clicking the "sign up" button on our website: www.titanbooks.com